HOOSIER HONOR

HOOSIER HONOR

*Bob Knight and
Academic Success
at Indiana University*

Robert Paul Sulek

Foreword by Charles V. Willie

PRAEGER

New York
Westport, Connecticut
London

Library of Congress Cataloging-in-Publication Data

Sulek, Robert Paul.
   Hoosier honor: Bob Knight and academic
success at Indiana University / Robert Paul Sulek.
      p.   cm.
   Includes bibliographical references.
   ISBN: 0–275–93447–0 (alk. paper)
   1. Indiana University—Basketball. 2. Knight, Bobby.
3. Basketball—United States—Coaches. I. Title.
GV885.43.I53S85   1990
796.323'63'09772255—dc20   89–38798

For
Nancy, Magdalene, Thaddeus . . .
the rest of our family,
and Mom

Contents

Photographs follow page 57

Tables

Foreword

This study of academic support services for student-athletes is timely and important. Having confessed their fault and culpability, colleges and universities must now do something positive about the education of student-athletes. Otherwise, they will be condemned as youth abusers. The record of their exploitation of student-athletes in inter-collegiate sports cries out for immediate reform.

Recent studies of student-athletes reveal that only one-fifth to one-third graduate from college. Among their classmates, about one out of every two who enrolls in an institution of higher education receives a degree. Why the discrepancy between degree attainment for student-athletes and other students? Robert Sulek believes the reason for this discrepancy lies not so much with the student-athletes as with the institutions in which they matriculate.

Many student-athletes dream of big things in the big leagues, but these dreams are seldom fulfilled for most of them. In the words of an old fraternity hymn, "College days swiftly pass" and athletic glories fade fast. The probability of a student-athlete gaining a position on a professional athletic team is small, and so are the earnings and opportunities for those who miss out. Even among the successful, injuries may end a promising career. Without a professional sports contract, without a college degree, and with uncultivated academic skills, famous student-athletes quickly become invisible rejects who are unable to make it in a complex postindustrial society.

Some colleges and universities are beginning to do something about the low rates of graduation among student-athletes. For example, a program has been introduced by the Center for the Study of Sports in

Society at Northeastern University to help former student-athletes in the major and minor leagues to continue their studies and receive a college degree. It is a worthy program to be sure, but it is of little help to the student-athlete who exhausts years of eligibility for competition in varsity intercollegiate sports, does not receive a bachelor's degree, and is passed over by recruiters for professional athletic teams.

Some colleges and universities are beginning to take corrective actions so that the hyphenated scholar, the student-athlete, is in reality a student and an athlete — not one or the other but *both*. The problem is that most colleges and universities that have been caught up in the practice of exploiting student-athletes do not know what to do. The easy way out of the dilemma is to blame the victim.

Bob Knight and the Athletic Department at Indiana University have refused to participate in the deceptive practice of blaming and bashing the student-athletes and thereby exonerating their institution. They have initiated and institutionalized a structure and process that encourages the student-athletes to honor their compounded status on the college campus.

The value of the Sulek study is in its demonstration that rhetoric alone will not do. Staff such as "Buzz" Kurpius must be retained. Often before or after practice, Sulek tells us, she appears on the courtside and beckons a basketball player or two over to discuss some academic matters. Buzz is like a watchdog. She monitors everything the student-athletes do. She and her staff are responsible for helping them become and remain students in good standing. She is also the student-athletes' friend. Her message is clear and straightforward: "You must go to class." Those who falter incur her wrath. Coach Knight fully supports her approach. Some of the athletes call their treatment at Indiana University "hard-love."

These student-athletes, Sulek reports, are not stronger in academic potential than those who enroll in other schools that have a history of producing winning teams. Yet he states that "an amazingly high percentage" of Indiana University varsity basketball players graduate. He attributes this outcome in part to the philosophy and character of Coach Knight, but he adds that these characteristics can be found in others. Moreover, institutional tradition has a great deal to do with whether one is honored for being both a student and an athlete. How to accomplish this duality effectively is what this book is about.

Sulek's study of academic support services for student-athletes is not a study in remediation methods. It is a study in the effective functioning of expectation. The effective schools movement has emphasized the importance of expectation in the learning process. Students expected to learn often learn. But expectations must be backed up with an effective delivery system. This study describes and analyzes such a system for student-athletes that has been tried, tested, and not found wanting. The outcome is something of value that can be, and deserves to be, replicated.

An important contribution of this study is that it shows public and private colleges and universities that have the will to educate student-athletes the way to accomplish this goal. Having read Sulek's study about the wonderful academic accomplishments of these athletes, one no longer should support the hypothesis that any are unwilling and unworthy students.

Charles V. Willie
Harvard University

Acknowledgments

The author wishes to thank those who helped to shape this work.

Dr. Charles Vert Willie of Harvard University is a close friend, advisor, and personal sociologist. His philosophy enables us to realize the importance of learning from diverse groups. His spirit burns with the fire and strength of a thousand sufferings. If only everyone could know him, the world would move.

Randy Michael Testa served as editor, running partner, and religious touchstone. Our runs along the Charles River filled my mind with the sacredness of the Amish, the importance of the deviant voice, and the meaning of being a true teacher.

All the labors of this book were softened by the trio of friends who never wavered in the strength of their devotion and general fullness they give to my life as brothers. They are: John Sterling — the gambler and sports fanatic with heart; Andy Gray — the Irish runner of wisdom; and Steve Piltch — the whirlwind of activity and sensitivity.

The project would have little meaning, inspiration, and chance of completion without Nancy Traina Sulek. Her faith and love in me were the driving force in having the story told properly. Where once there was a void in my life, she now occupies that space.

Introduction

When I was 13 years old, my older brother and I retreated into the nearby woods and found a long, straight, and sturdy tree. We chopped it down with an ax and skinned off the branches. What remained was about 14 feet of yet-to-be basketball support, 4 feet of which would later be driven into the ground. We dragged the prized tree about a mile to our backyard and then attached a wooden three-by-three backboard. When we hoisted it up into the hole, we looked like John Wayne and his fellow marines in the movie *The Sands of Iwo Jima* raising the American flag. We were proud of our work and played basketball all day on our new court. Within a week the grass was worn away, and the outlines of a large, all-dirt basketball court could be detected. During rain or snow we covered the area beneath the net with flattened cardboard boxes so that the ball would fall on a dry surface.

I played four to eight hours every day for almost 25 years. I guess there are many others with a similar basketball history. The game was and still is a part of me. But for lack of athletic ability, I had to substitute intensity, hustle, and team play.

In college I scored two points in my entire career and drank Pepsi to celebrate my high-scoring outburst. I relived the moment over and over, embellishing the drama with time. The reality was that I was the thirteenth man on a 13-man squad. Like many overachieving and underqualified players, I sat on the bench and became a cerebral player. Where there was skill lacking, my mind saw small things to compensate. I actually became a better player as I got older. Well into my thirties, I continued to improve even though my physical skills began to wane. Positioning now afforded me rebounds rather than jumping ability. Head fakes brought continual fouls. Defensively I could cover good players by cutting the floor and running angles rather than large arcs.

Eventually injuries end the careers of all old basketball players. It is a game that requires fresh and strong legs. Injury and age turn old players into coaches. Sometimes mediocre players become excellent coaches because they compensate for their lack of physical ability — demanding, aggressive, intense, and hard-working coaches. Coaches value defense because defense takes courage. Defensive players have heart. Anyone can play offense. Anyone can shoot the ball. Good defense stops good offense. Defense wins games.

Nowhere is defense played as it is played at Indiana University (IU). The clawing, physical, man-to-man variety. This defense slowly strangles the minds of opposing offensive players like the coils of a python around its prey. This defense is more than one player acting alone. It is a well-trained unit functioning in unison. A probe into the defense affects every player — physically and personally. This Indiana defense is one of great pride and courage.

For an opponent, a player, a coach, or a fan, this Hoosier defense is arguably the best. Not good or above average. The best. Its architect must be a man who felled and skinned a tree. A man with limitations who learns to compensate. A man coaching a team with limitations. More than a man: a teacher and a mentor.

His basketball success does not need to be documented. Instead, his success in graduating student-athletes is documented here. Too little attention has been placed on this important success and on the programs and people behind that success.

It will be easy to chronicle the programs, but the man that drives them will prove to be a challenge.

I know the man, but I don't know him.

It is this backdrop and this personal history that have brought me to the steps of Assembly Hall in Bloomington, Indiana, to research the success of Indiana University's basketball team in graduating student-athletes under the tenure of Coach Robert Montgomery Knight.

This research first details the failure of college sports: failure in the numbers not graduating, failure in the exploitation and abuse of athletes, failure in providing for the future of players, and above all, failure in both spirit and philosophy.

I came to IU armed with only a copy of Dostoevsky's *The Brothers Karamazov*. I know that a link exists between the "hard-love" described by the character Father Zossima and the success of Coach Bobby Knight.

Knight's love is evident. It is difficult, frustrating, demanding, and depressing at times. His love is powerful, deep, caring, compassionate, and understanding. The love is key to the phenomenal success of his program. It is this love, the people, and processes I will explore.

An Indiana Player

An Indiana basketball player can come in any size, shape or color. There is no common denominator except a love for the game and a desire to get the most out of his abilities. He is not only proud of his strengths but understands his weaknesses. He is first of all concerned with the good of his team and knows that individual recognition will come through team excellence.

Hoosier: The Indiana Athletic Review, 21 January 1989, 6

1

Genesis of the Study: The Problem

> Men reject their prophets and slay them, but they love their martyrs and honour those whom they have slain.
>
> *The Brothers Karamazov*

My academic problems started with my beginning years in grammar school. Like the other 23 million illiterates today, and the 35 million functional illiterates, I never learned to read, write and compute.... The courses were selected for me by the athletic director and coaches at Creighton. And, of course, these courses were easy courses, such as the theory of first aid, the theory of tennis, and basketball — courses that require not one lofty thought.... In fact, I thought of suicide many times. What Creighton University did to me — I forgive them because I have no vindictiveness.[1]

Kevin Ross, former college basketball player — without a diploma — is currently in jail, a product of frustration and exploitation. University of Maryland All-American basketball player Len Bias is dead of cocaine-induced cardiac arrest. Tulane University has shut down its basketball program because of a point-shaving scandal. The North Carolina State University basketball program under Coach Jim Valvano has recently come under scrutiny by the school's administration. The Wolfpack team has been extremely successful in winning basketball games, but has an abysmal record in keeping and graduating its players. The focus of this book is not to peruse substance abuse or athlete exploitation but to assist current basketball players to graduate.

Black sociologist Harry Edwards (University of California at Berkeley) claims that 75 percent of all Black athletes never graduate from college.[2] College basketball players miss as much as 35 percent of their classes during the spring semester. Notes, quizzes, homework, and tests are consequently missed.

DIFFICULTIES OF THE STUDENT-ATHLETE

James Rhatigan (1984), vice president for student affairs and dean of students at Wichita State University, claims that athletes in Division I colleges (nearly 300 schools with the largest enrollment or those schools playing a schedule consisting of mostly other Division I schools) basketball programs face an unfavorable set of demanding circumstances. In the second semester of the academic year, most teams play eight to ten "away" games. This means that players miss nearly 15 class days out of 75 in a semester, or approximately 20 percent of all spring classes. If the team is 1 of the 64 schools in the postseason NCAA (National Collegiate Athletic Association) tournament, another 2 to 6 percent can be added to missed time. This adds up to a lot of missed notes, quizzes, and tests. There is rarely a holiday break for the athletes or an opportunity to earn money during school breaks since most schools play in holiday tournaments and practice, view game films, and work on individual weaknesses during this time. "Now add to this," says Rhatigan, "the rigors of extensive travel. Travel is unsettling for many people. Sleeping in a strange bed and eating at unusual hours take a toll, as does waiting in airports and coping with misplaced baggage, books left behind, and uncomfortably close connections."[3] Rhatigan also points out that with a 28-game schedule, pressure on the athlete to win, the fans' belief that the athlete is a pampered pseudoprofessional, and unrealistic time demands placed by the coaches, the student-athlete is left to feel at times lost, unimportant, and harried.

Many high school basketball players arrive academically unprepared for college and have difficulty in catching up. The median percentage for special admits (i.e., academically weak) football and basketball players for all Division I colleges is 37. These players have special academic needs and deficiencies.[4] Many student-athletes have serious problems being full-time students and big-time college athletes. The problem is particularly acute for highly competitive programs in football and basketball. This book is for them.

The average Division I basketball program includes provisions for tutors and study halls. Usually the daily attendance of the players is monitored through a weekly checklist for each class instructor, which, when signed, is then sent to the academic support staff. However, the combination of excellent basketball and the consistent graduation of student-athletes is lacking in all but a tiny minority of NCAA schools. Most schools either cannot win or cannot graduate players or cannot do either. According to the 1987 NCAA Division I study, less than half of the basketball players in Division I schools actually earn their diplomas.[5]

Ira M. Heyman, chancellor of the University of California at Berkeley, writes, "Most [college athletes] end college worse off than when they started. . . . They do not have a degree. They have not developed into well-rounded, capable adults. They have not prepared themselves at all for life after sports."[6] Heyman feels the solution rests in acquiring detailed information about the athletic programs in this country. These data would focus on what is currently happening on our nation's campuses regarding sports. There is little research in this area. Two new studies in progress are being completed by the NCAA: One provides an in-depth look at the lives of student-athletes, whereas the other is a five-year study of Proposition 48 (the high school requirements to play college sports).

Indiana University has made a commitment to graduating student-athletes. Its reputation is grounded in excellence. Coach Bob Knight has been at Indiana University since 1971. He embodies that excellence. In an Indiana University basketball publication, Knight comments on his basketball program:

Very few schools have combined athletics and academics as successfully as Indiana, yet we take as much pride in the accomplishments of our players after they have left IU as we do in all their achievements here in school. All but two of our four-year players have completed or are finishing degrees. . . .

I have always made it clear that an education is the top priority for our players; basketball is secondary. But, just as the University offers exceptional educational opportunities in all fields, it also offers a basketball program without equal.[7]

Knight has won the NCAA championship three times. He has been the U.S. Olympic team coach and Coach of the Year and is the most winning coach in the Big Ten Conference. He is regarded by many of his peers as the finest basketball coach with regard to designing game strategy, motivating players, and organizing college practices.

IU is a public institution with an outstanding basketball program that graduates an extremely high percentage of its players. In this, Indiana is doing something most winning basketball programs are not doing. College Division I basketball players have a predominance of Black players compared with other intercollegiate sports.[8] "Blacks make up only 12 percent of the total U.S. population. But in NCAA Division I, 36 percent of the football players and 52 percent of the basketball players are black," writes columnist Art Spander.[9] The University of Georgia has a 4 percent graduation rate for Black athletes; Memphis State University has not graduated a Black athlete in the past decade.[10] The University of Nevada at Las Vegas (UNLV) has had difficulty in graduating basketball players.

ACADEMIC PROGRESS OF ATHLETES

Research literature describing student-athletes is inconsistent. Ewing (1975) found athletes had worse attitudes and study habits than nonathletes. Sowa and Gressard (1983) found that participants in varsity athletics at the collegiate level had significantly lower achievement in developmental tasks than nonathletes.

Purdy, Eitzen, and Hufnagel (1982) studied 2,000 college athletes over a ten-year time period at a major western university. They concluded that athletes were academically less prepared for college and they achieved far less than the general student population when enrolled. In particular, they found the graduation rate of Black athletes was 21 percent, whereas the rate for Caucasian athletes was 35 percent. The graduation rate for the general student population in their study was 47 percent. They also found athletes admitted with a high school grade-point average (GPA) under 2.5 graduated at a rate of 3 percent. In summary, Purdy et al. found that athletes

> entered with poorer academic backgrounds, received lower grades than their non-athletic peers, and fewer of them graduated.... There is evidence that athletes in ... basketball have a relatively low probability of receiving an education compared to non-athletes.[11]

Student needs appear secondary to the need of the university to gain and maintain a winning program.[12] A study at the University of Nevada at Las Vegas followed the academic progress of 41 basketball players from 1978 to 1981.[13] The researchers focused on course work and transcripts. The Physical Education (PE) Department ranked first as a source of course credits (30 percent of all credits for basketball players). The most frequent physical education courses taken were Intercollegiate Sports, Workshop in PE, Conditioning, and Fieldwork in PE.

Black athletes appear to experience more difficulty in graduating than White athletes, according to Spivey and Jones (1975), Oates (1979), and Underwood (1980). In contrast, Bostic (1979) found that all athletes, regardless of race, face academic problems different from the general student population. He found no differences between Black and White athletes. Others see special difficulties for Blacks.

Contradictions arise concerning overall graduation rates for athletes. Pilapil, Stecklein, and Lui (1970), Billick (1973), and Michener (1976) found that athletes graduate at a higher rate than nonathletes. These studies conflict with the findings of Webb (1968), Harrison (1976), and Benagh (1976) who concluded that athletes graduate at a lower rate than nonathletes. The same contradictions result when GPA is used as a variable for athletes versus nonathletes.

Current data appear to clear up most of the contradictions of earlier studies. This research is headed by the NCAA "1989 Survey of Student-Athletes." The study finds that the high school preparation of basketball players is weaker than the general incoming student body. These college basketball players do have lower GPAs than their cohorts and also have less time for student work than other extracurricular students. This study is examined in the next chapter.

Bylaw 5–1–(j) is the NCAA's attempt to confront the problem. It demands academic preparedness of high school seniors.

BYLAW 5–1–(J): THE NCAA'S SOLUTION

> What seems to you bad within you will grow purer from the very fact of your observing it in yourself.
>
> *The Brothers Karamazov*

Bylaw 5–1–(j) states that to be eligible an incoming student-athlete must have a 2.0 GPA in 11 high school core courses (English, mathematics, social studies, etc.) and a combined 700 score or better on the Scholastic Aptitude Test (SAT). Student-athletes not meeting both of these standards must sit out their freshman year of athletics.

Klitgaard (1983, 1984) found that if Bylaw 5–1–(j) had been enacted in 1976, at least 60 percent of college-admitted Black athletes would have been ineligible. Outcry in response to Bylaw 5–1–(j) was quick and furious.

Historically many Black college presidents and civil rights leaders objected to the bylaw on two principles: (1) no Blacks participated in the formulation of the bylaw and (2) the 700 total SAT score was arbitrary. Black college presidents whose entire student body often average under 700 on the SAT found the figure discriminatory. Weldon Jackson, Black vice president of Morehouse College, had less than a 700 SAT score as a high school senior. Jackson subsequently graduated Phi Beta Kappa from Morehouse and with a Ph.D. from Harvard University. Also, complaints were registered by Black leaders about making basketball "Whiter" by benching the Black players. Many athletes successfully competed in sports while attending college and graduated without a 700 SAT in the prebylaw days.

The NCAA commissioned a study that showed that, had the rules been in force in 1981, nearly 60 percent of football and basketball recruits would have been ineligible.

But when it took effect in 1986, after a three-year warning period, high schools had cleaned up their acts. . . 13 percent of basketball

players were ineligible — proof that athletes perform academically when asked.[14]

Jesse Stone, Jr., the president of Southern University, said, "The
end result of all this is the Black athlete has been too good. If it [bylaw]
is followed to its logical conclusion, we say to our youngsters, 'Let the
White boy win once in a while.' This has set the Black athlete back 25
or 30 years. The message is that White schools no longer want Black
athletes."[15] This sentiment is supported by Black coach John Chaney
at Temple University who feels that Black kids are being used as
"guinea pigs."

Black sociologist Harry Edwards (1984) has defended Bylaw 5–1–
(j), claiming that, first, the rule establishes standards of high school
preparation for college athletic eligibility; second, athletes must
develop academically; third, Blacks can achieve 700 SAT scores; and
finally, the bylaw is not racist.

"The NCAA will know by 1994 if it has successfully bullied high
schools into educating the nation's young. . . . More than 4,000
teenagers likely will have felt the sting of Proposal 48 by then. Nearly
all of them will be Black."[16] The number of Blacks involved in Proposition 48 (basketball victims) is staggering: 58 out of 60 in 1987. These
athletes will lose one year of basketball eligibility by sitting out their
freshman year.

Student-athletes have faced unique problems — exploitation, low
academic self-esteem, little free time for work or study, and the
fleeting dream of a professional basketball career. Many come from
inner-city public school systems and need counseling, remedial help,
and academic support. The conclusion that can be drawn is that
basketball players as a group will not succeed in college academics
unless a way can be found to help them.

METHODS OF ENTRY

The Indiana University figures involving basketball games won and
subsequent graduation of the athletes are staggering. Coach Knight's
16 years have produced three NCAA championships, a National In-

vitational Tournament (NIT) championship, a Pan-Am gold medal, an Olympic gold medal, and nearly a 75 percent winning average. More impressive than Knight's genius for coaching has been IU's astounding success rate in graduating basketball players (nearly 90 percent). Graduated players also have a documented success in business and the work force. Knight insists that the lessons learned in the preparation to become as good as possible in basketball are also transferable to job skills. Knight's character and personality are tied to a philosophy of hard work, perseverance, self-worth, and intensity. Knight perceives his job as a teacher and leader of young men rather than as a mere basketball coach.

Entry to the inner circles of basketball people is difficult for the researcher, and one can never speak or correspond directly with the head coach without intermediaries—secretaries, assistant coaches, and sports information directors.

I sent letters and made phone calls to anyone who might help me gain access to pertinent information. In June 1988 I attended a three-day coaching clinic by Coach Knight at Bloomington and stayed another week to meet coaches, players, academic support people, and others. This introductory phase was coupled with face-to-face meetings and brief exchanges with Knight. Appointments were then made to gather perceptions of the people to be interviewed. At the same time, letters to higher-ups in all crucial departments (i.e., basketball, academic support, and administration) were sent before my arrival. These letters included information and documents needed from the particular person or department. Finally, a "disclaimer" stating that the research was about a positive happening in college basketball—the successful graduation of players—was also included. I wanted to convey a relationship of trust. I also hoped to leave the impression that this book was to be a study about something good happening in sports—not an exposé meant to criticize the program and its people.

In spite of these precautions and preparations the following letter from Tates Locke, the assistant coach, arrived at my door three days before I would embark to Indiana:

> There must be some confusion regarding what you will be accomplishing during your visit here in Bloomington. We will not be in a position to personalize any visits and interviews with you. . . . You

will not receive the cooperation that I'm sure you'll need because
of our schedule.

If I have led you to believe otherwise I apologize.

Nevertheless, I decided to attend the clinic. On its first day, introductions were made to assistant coaches Joby Wright, Dan Dakich, and
Tates Locke. I would not get in the way but would be available if the
assistants found time to talk. Then Knight walked into the gymnasium
for the first of his series of presentations regarding various pieces of
basketball strategy, tactics, and philosophy.

At six feet five inches and over 200 pounds, Knight is a large man,
physically imposing. He has a reputation for being quick tempered,
with a razor-sharp tongue. A principled man, he believes in giving the
best of himself and expects the same from those in his charge. He is
exceptionally bright, quick-witted, and perceptive. His genius at basketball is universally acknowledged, and his troubles and temper have
been widely documented by an eager press: a confrontation with a
Puerto Rican policeman during the 1979 Pan American Games in
Puerto Rico; allegations that Knight stuffed a Louisiana State University fan into a garbage can during the 1981 Final Four NCAA Basketball Championships; the 1985 game during which Knight hurled a chair
across the floor; the 1987 Soviet team fiasco that resulted in Knight
pulling the IU team off the court with 15 minutes remaining in the
game because of a quarrel with officials; and finally, in 1988 Knight
grabbing IU player Steve Eyl and shoving him down on a bench.

With some uncertainty I approached Knight after his final address
to a crowd of 200 high school and college coaches. The exchange was
brief but pointed.

"I'm very busy this week. . . . I don't think we can help you on this
visit," Knight declared.

Nonetheless, I persisted and decided to work around the schedules
of the Indiana coaches and stay away from the players (as Knight had
instructed). There were plenty of people to interview—the entire
academic support staff, the registrar, physical education administrators, faculty, and students.

Word of these interviews and their friendly character reached Knight.
He granted an interview the next evening after his final lecture for the
basketball clinic. That evening arrived and after waiting for Knight to

finish signing autographs and exchange pleasantries with a handful of coaches, Knight walked within inches of me and disappeared into an office. He had stood me up for our first scheduled appointment.

The following morning another interview with Knight was re-scheduled for the same time as before, which was after the closing presentation of the day-long seminar. This time, after Knight had another round of well-wishers and picture-taking sessions, he beckoned me to a side office. In this room were several of Knight's cronies, and hence a short interview, at best, commenced:

Knight: What do you want? I don't have time today.

Sulek: I'll schedule around your time. I'm here for another five days and will be back in October, then December.

Knight: I have friends visiting here and want to spend time with them.

Sulek: I'll just explain what I'm doing here. My lifelong ambition as a basketball coach was to send a player to you. I had one good one — Mark Bryant — who is six feet nine inches and a high school All-American. We used all the Indiana drills. . .

Knight: How did I fuck that one up?

Sulek: You had no more scholarships that season 1984, and Mark was too poor to come without aid. I would like to repay you for the fine drills and inspiration I've learned over the years. I want to show a different side of you that the world doesn't know — the successful graduation rate of players and. . .

Knight: You can arrange to talk to the players through Kit [sports information director], and I'll try to meet you at the end of the week.

Sulek: Thanks, Coach.

A personal interview with Coach Knight never took place since Knight was off on a whirlwind of lectures and recruiting trips. How-ever, he had opened the door to procure all the necessary pieces — the players, the coaches, and the data.

I spent the next week talking to as many people as possible, becom-ing known, explaining the project, reassuring doubters, and laying the groundwork for the book. Though a willing ally, Buzz Kurpius, director of the Academic Support Group, was nonetheless reluctant to relinquish the computer file on the basketball players through Knight's tenure. These files contained majors, GPAs, high school rank, SAT/ACT (American College Test) scores, racial breakdowns, and graduation rates. They would be a necessary part of the study, but I needed Knight's explicit permission to access the data.

I also asked the people I interviewed to suggest others for future interviews who would have perceptions about the academic success of Indiana University. In this fashion, names, home telephone numbers, and addresses were obtained for the next visit.

One source of documentation for the book came from the sports information director's office. It contained newspapers and magazine clippings dating back to Knight's arrival at Indiana. Also, Buzz Kurpius held all record-keeping documents for the players as well as all handouts given to the athletes. Basketball yearbooks, athletic handbooks, and NCAA studies were found at Alumni Hall. Photographs were taken of the campus, buildings, gym, archways, and people interviewed. I sent these photos back to those interviewed along with a letter thanking them and highlighting the experience.

From the beginning, this book was meant to focus on something good in college basketball. My focus was on success. Not every story at IU is a positive one; however, these are not detailed here. Knight has probably driven off some players that possibly did not achieve either academically or athletically as he expected. The system at IU is rather rigid and paternalistic. This study will focus on the process and people that generated the overwhelming success in the graduation of players.

In a letter written July 1, 1988, I expressed my new-found understanding of the IU situation to Coach Knight:

> I interviewed several dozen players, coaches, academic support staff, and administrators. My respect and admiration for you was, I believe, at the highest level possible, but after listening to interview after interview I began to realize your true greatness was not in basketball, but in your care, compassion, and concern for your players and friends. Tates told me that "if you had Bobby Knight for a friend, you only need one friend"—what greater

compliment can you receive? Several people gave me confidential accounts of your kindness and generosity. . . . I will show a side of Knight that the world doesn't realize. I will focus on the success, care, and compassion in the graduation of basketball players.

I'm looking forward to my next visit late fall. Hopefully, we can get together for an interview at that time.

To Assistant Coach Tates Locke, the following letter was also sent on July 1 along with a Herman Hesse novel:

Thank you so much for your time and honesty in our conversation. . . . Have you had an opportunity to read Hesse? If you like this book try his *Demian*, and *Narcissus and Goldman*. . . . Tates, please come and visit us in Boston if you get the chance. . . . If I can do anything personally for you or the IU team, please let me know. I was a Knight fan before I came out for a visit, but I never realized what great friends he had.

I sent letters to Buzz and others, thanking them, requesting more materials, setting up second visits, and establishing good working relations. While I compiled data, transcribed tapes, and wrote observations and perceptions, letters and data from those interviewed began to arrive.

Coach Knight adopted a new attitude toward my project in his September note. "If I am at home, I'll be glad to spend some time with you. Perhaps you and Hammel [author Bob Hammel] and I can go out to eat while we are there," Knight's letter began. Access was finally granted to the inner circles.

During the second visit at Indiana, the registrar provided an "in-house" analysis of the *1987–88 Fall Enrollment Report* and a historical overview. There still remained two problems—an interview with a major basketball player and access to the IU basketball player records. The player, Jay Edwards, was in a drug rehabilitation center, and the coaches requested that I wait until winter after "he [Jay] has a chance to get himself together." Buzz was stalling on the player files; so I made an appeal directly to Knight:

Sulek: Coach, Buzz says I need your permission to get the records for the players.

Knight: You can't have them. I don't want any of these kids exposed.

Sulek: Coach, I have to show that you get kids just like everyone else. Some come with 700 SATs, others 1,000. Some are in the bottom of the high school rank and some top ten. People will say they are all White and bright kids. They'll say Indiana only graduates them because they all major in physical education. I need the records to show that's not the case.

Knight: You can have them, but don't use any of their names.

A week later a detailed chart with every player ever to play for Bobby Knight, complete with all relevant academic data, arrived in my mail. I was the first researcher to acquire this information. This chart had comparisons between IU cohorts, college basketball players (from an NCAA study), high school students (from a national study), and the IU basketball players. It was then possible to document the outstanding success of this program.

All interviews were broken down into several categories: assistant basketball coaches, Physical Education Department administration, the press and print media, current players, former players, academic support staff, tutors, Indiana University administrators, faculty, students, friends of Knight, Buzz Kurpius, and Bobby Knight. A few notables were interviewed two or three times because of their special importance to the research (i.e., Knight, Kurpius, Pratter, and Downing). An author of a recent Knight biography, Joan Mellen, was interviewed by phone several times. (See the Appendix.)

By my third visit in December 1988, trust and a friendly relationship had developed between me and all the critical figures of the study. Documents were relatively easy to access and could even be obtained by a long-distance phone call. And finally, Coach Knight, returning from a day-long hunting excursion, granted an extended interview in which he addressed all my questions patiently and in great detail. Further trips to Bloomington, Muncie, and some other smaller towns in Indiana were undertaken to complete interviews from the players.

In retrospect, I wish that I had asked Coach Knight some questions that have become more important over the course of this past year (i.e., about the new Proposition 42, which is a stricter version of

Proposition 48; the SAT controversy; etc.). In addition, my understanding of Knight's motivations and philosophy would have been more complete, had I been privy to meetings between Knight and his subordinates, the academic support staff, and the players. My information derives from one-on-one interviews between myself and Bobby Knight, as well as my research and interviews with other people, and data given to me. I wanted to be a silent observer — the "fly on the wall" — but that turned out to be impossible.

NOTES

1. U.S., Congress, House, "Testimony of Kevin Ross to U.S. Congress," *Oversight on College Athletic Programs*, 98th Cong., 2d sess., 26 June 1984, pp. 3–5.

2. Richard Lapchick, *Fractured Focus — Sport as a Reflection of Society* (Lexington, Mass.: Lexington Books, 1986).

3. James J. Rhatigan, "Serving Two Masters: The Plight of the College Student-Athlete," *NASPA Journal*, Summer 1984, 43.

4. National Collegiate Athletic Association, *1987 Division I Academic Reporting Compilation* (Mission, Kans.: NCAA, June 1988), 5.

5. Ibid., table 5.

6. Ira M. Heyman, "NCAA Forum," *NCAA News*, 8 July 1987, 6.

7. "Letter from Coach Knight," *Indiana University Basketball — A Winning Tradition* (Bloomington: Indiana University Printing Services; Rheitone, Inc., Indianapolis, 1987), 4.

8. Harry Edwards, "Educating Black Athletes — NCAA's Rule 48," *Educational Digest*, January 1984, 22–25.

9. Art Spander, "Can Sports Tear Down Racial Barricades?" *Sporting News*, 13 February 1989, 5.

10. Lapchick, *Fractured Focus*, 2.

11. Dean A. Purdy, D. S. Eitzen, and R. Hufnagel, "Are Athletes Also Students? The Educational Attainment of College Athletes," *Social Problems*, April 1982, 445.

12. J. Renick, "The Use and Misuse of College Athletes," *Journal of Higher Education* 54 (1974): 542–52.

13. J. Raney, T. Knapp, and M. Small, "Pass One for the Gipper: Student-Athletes and University Course Work," *Arena Review*, November 1983, 53–60.

14. "Some Are Making the Grade," *USA Today*, 4 April 1988, 2C.

15. Jesse Stone, Jr., "Black Colleges Threaten to Quit NCAA," *New York Times*, 13 January 1983, 1.

16. "Some Are Making the Grade," 2C.

2

Bobby Knight

There are three powers, three powers alone, able to conquer, to hold captive forever the conscience . . . those forces are miracle, mystery and authority.

The Brothers Karamazov

The trip by car from Indianapolis to Bloomington is only 51 miles, but in that hour a new world emerges. Rock singer John Cougar Mellencamp (Indiana native) is heard across the FM radio dial. What impresses one on Route 37 are the miles and miles of land: farmland, flat, open land — beautiful land. Just 15 miles out on the journey is Larry Bird's car dealership. It has a parquet floor just like the Boston Garden and a life-size cutout of Bird in a Boston Celtic familiar green number "33" uniform. The road winds into Indiana heartland. Farms and accompanying homes have outdoor basketball courts — basket and rim usually attached to a telephone pole, sometimes to a garage, or even to store-bought metal poles with rectangular backboards. Often one sees a tree dragged down from the woods, shaved straight and mounted ten feet tall. There is a rubber Wilson basketball lying out in the yard where it was probably left as a mother beckoned her teenage offspring to chores or mealtime. Basketball is much more than a game here in this land.

The linchpin of Indiana hoopla and roundball is Indiana University in Bloomington. Giant arches mark the entrance to the main campus. The buildings of the central campus make up but a tiny portion of 1,850 wooded acres, 32,700 students, and 3,000 full-time faculty. In 1820 the Indiana State Seminary began on these grounds, and eight years later it became Indiana College. There is Ernie Pyle Hall, which houses the

School of Journalism. Beck Chapel, petite and steepled, taken from some fairy-tale setting. Libraries, museums, fountains, cyclotrons, and restored homes dot the acreage. There are even parking lots, grass, trees, lakes, and joggers. Tucked in the northern corner of this complex is the throne of college basketball: Assembly Hall.

Harry Pratter's wife set the cooking timer for 90 minutes — the amount of time allotted for our interview. Pratter, Law Professor Emeritus at Indiana University, recently had a heart attack and was recovering at home. He sat on his couch and wore a black beret and a button-down sweater. Coach Knight asked him to negotiate a contract for one of his IU players who was going into the NBA. An appeal was also made to Pratter to come to practice, accompany the team on road trips, and address the team before or after practice. He is the type of man Knight wants as an example for his students.

"Knight has a great respect for education and intelligence. He respects minds and has a feel for smart people, and broadly educated people appeal to him," Pratter remarked in our interview.

World-renowned cellist Janos Starker addressed the IU team before practice in early 1985. Bob Hammel, sports editor of the *Herald-Telephone* in Bloomington, reported Starker's conversation with the Indiana basketball team: "When I received the telephone call [from Knight] asking me to come to talk to you, I was startled. Almost as much as you are: 'What is a cellist doing talking to us?'"[1] The only question, however, in Starker's mind now turned to, "Why wasn't I asked sooner?" Starker continued:

> There is no question that people who succeed in any field, sport or art, will only succeed if they have taken care of training their brain. That's the constantly reoccurring issue in the sports activities: that one would prefer honing the skills of finding the basket. But he can do it far better if he finds out that if I do it this way, what happens to my other arm muscles?
>
> I spent a lifetime trying to understand the underlying basic principles that make it possible for someone to use body, arms and then the head. . . and to make it consistent is what we are all trying to get in every field. That's where brain process, analysis, and the total dedication, in preparation as well as while it is in progress, and the discipline that is required.[2]

Starker wanted the players to realize that as he tried to maximize what nature gave him, so must they. "What is necessary in my profession is no different from yours. . . . After a performance, if I remember that in the second movement, my mind drifted for a moment. . . I am ashamed."[3] He spoke of discipline and concentration in the same breath and the same sentences. Hammel's article concluded by Starker telling a story of three cellists who died. On arriving at the gates of Heaven they were asked for their credentials before entering. The first two were denied admittance even though they were quite distinguished. However, the third, on being asked for his credentials, replied that his teacher was Starker. "You can get in. You have already been through hell."[4] The IU players and Knight laughed, realizing that the parallels didn't need to be elaborated.

Coach Knight has invited many successful people to speak to his players. According to Harry Pratter, Knight has tried to focus on those "who were involved in athletics and are now just as successful in doing something else." Bill Bradley, a college All-American basketball player at Princeton University, is now a U.S. senator in New Jersey. Dick Vermeil was a brilliant coach for the Philadelphia Eagles and now is a successful broadcaster on television. These men, along with sports greats Willie Davis, Red Auerbach, Willis Reed, Paul Horning, Bill Parcell, Wayne Embry, and many others, have spoken to the Indiana University players at one time or another.

Pratter recalls that President Woodrow Wilson was a football coach at one time. Many Harvard people, including President Derek Bok, had coaching backgrounds as well. Basketball has an "aesthetic aspect to it that closely resembles a choreographed ballet," Pratter believes. One finds physical grace, effortless movements, and deep underlying planned thought. For Knight the complexities of basketball are a challenge to the mind. It takes an understanding of people and the intellect to transform the game into the music and beauty. Pratter further believes that "every moment for every player there is a right thing and a wrong thing to do" (like Starker's ashamed moment). For Knight the players must develop a feeling and an instinct for the right thing. Pratter also thinks that no one has a deeper understanding than Knight for the interaction of the mind and sport. For Knight (like Arturo Toscanini — the conductor) a violent temper comes to the fore in the teaching or berating of a violinist or point guard.

Knight is "relentless in his pursuit of excellence" and has an infinite attention to detail. Coach Knight can stop play at basketball practice and amazingly recount where all ten players were. He says, "It is a complicated game and we don't just run up and down the floor. There is anticipation like a chess game. Good players will think about three or four steps in advance. They are sensitive to the next development. They have a vision of the game." Pratter explains that no one would tolerate a slip of the hand by a heart surgeon or an error in judgment by an airplane pilot. Therefore, for Knight not to tolerate error and lack of concentration on the playing floor, in the classroom, or in business is understandable. Knight demands their best at all times. He demands and expects more of them than they expect of themselves. In Knight's view, to succeed is not equated with winning basketball games but with effort and personal self-respect to do their best.

The basketball floor is Knight's classroom. Lectures take place daily. Mistakes are not tolerated and are corrected. Knight has said of his players:

> I want him [a student] to go away and say, well, I learned more in basketball than in any class I took at Indiana. Basketball was by far the most educational experience that I had when I was at Indiana. And if that kid says, well, Chemistry 401 was my best, then I want to find out what the hell that guy is teaching in Chemistry 401 because I ought to be teaching it in basketball.[5]

Knight believes that a university can succeed without a basketball team but not, for example, without a mathematics department. Hence, Knight's "students" must be successful on another level beyond basketball. This level involves a respect for the university and the diploma as well as success beyond graduation in business or whatever. These goals are fulfilled by an insistence to try, a commitment to succeed, and an intolerant attitude toward failure. Failure is measured only against the self — the demands one makes on himself or herself and the respect for self.

Knight has a genuine respect for what a university is all about. The players are taught this respect. The first point of contact is attendance. Attendance is quantifiable. The players have to be students and they have to attend class. In an interview with David England, Knight commented:

> We simply demand as much of a kid in the classroom as we do on the basketball court. If a kid doesn't attend class, then he is a problem, and he does not play basketball. It's just that simple. Our kids *know* with certainty what the rules are and the consequences of breaking them. . . .
>
> I don't think you can take a kid who does not go to class or who does not want to work to accomplish what he can in the classroom and then get out of him athletically what you have to get out of him. I don't think there is *any* way. And, by the same token, I think a kid who competes and executes well athletically can be a hell of a good student, too.[6]

The symbol of learning for Knight as well as the university's most tangible asset is the "book." The book captures the commitment for learning. All players must develop a devotion to books. Knight has committed himself to books. He is an avid reader and a Civil War buff. Ulysses S. Grant is one of his favorite characters in history. When I inquired about Knight's passion for Grant, the answer contained a 15-minute history lesson.

For every 100 men under Grant's command, there were ten casualties. For every 100 under Lee's command, there were 17 casualties. Who is your favorite writer of the Civil War? [Bruce Catton.] He's from Virginia. Most writers of the Civil War are Southerners. Their accounts are biased and favor Lee. There is a veneration of Lee. Grant never lost a battle. He was a poor president but had a special moment in history. He had the first Union victories. Lee's genius is a fallacy. Longstreet advised Lee not to make a stand at Gettysburg and Lee ignored the advice.

When I asked Knight if he visited the battlefields, he replied:

Most of them. But you should read *Grant and Lee*, published by IU Press, to get a balanced view of these men by a British colonel. Grant himself was a great writer and wrote his autobiography under severe conditions since he was suffering from cancer of the throat.

In Knight's home, near his favorite reading chair there are two piles of books on each side, reaching up to arm level. His tastes are wide and varied from Sun-Tzu's *The Art of War* (written 500 years before the Christian era in China — this book is Knight's favorite "basketball" book for tactics, strategy, and coaching) to Gore Vidal's *Burr.* He sits by himself at the front of the team's chartered jet for away games, always with book in hand. It is not only the players that he tries to influence but also the assistant coaches. Jim Crews, former player at IU and also former assistant coach, idolized Knight and tried to copy his style as head coach at Evansville University. Knight was reading a particular mystery-spy novel on a road trip. On the return trip Crews was seen devouring the same book.

Knight has always read for enjoyment. His mother was a third-grade teacher and "there were always books around the house." His grade school had a yearly reading contest to name the top ten readers in school. Knight says, "It was always me and nine girls in the top ten." Knight recalls walking to the library in Ohio as a small boy to get his first library card. As a boy he read John Tunnis, Chip Hilton, the Hardy Boys, and American biographies. Later, as an undergraduate, he studied history and political science.

Young Knight was the only son of Pat and Hazel Knight from Orrville, Ohio (population 8,500). Bob's father worked at the nearby railroad and died of leukemia in 1970. His mother passed away in 1988.

When Knight was 16 years old, he wrote an autobiography entitled "It's Been a Great Life (So Far)." In this unpublished journal, he listed three future goals: going to college, joining the service, and becoming a basketball coach.

After completing his undergraduate career at Ohio State University with a major in history, Knight planned to attend law school at University of California at Los Angeles (UCLA). Instead, he enlisted in the army. Soon after basic training was completed, Private First-Class Knight became the youngest head basketball coach in the country at the age of 24 at West Point. He was to become the most successful coach in the history of the army with a record of 120–50 (wins-losses) and four (NIT) appearances in six seasons.

In 1972 at the age of 30, Knight accepted the head basketball coaching position at Indiana University. Before he arrived the team barely drew 4,000 people to a game, and the season prior to Knight's arrival, dissension had torn the team apart. The next 17 years is a tale of unparalleled success. After three NCAA national championships, there are no seats available in Assembly Hall, with a seating capacity of 17,500 for any of the games. Knight just passed his 500 career-win total as well as the most wins of any coach in Big Ten history. Most people (even his critics) feel the season 1988–89 is Knight's best coaching performance ever. In early 1989 *Sporting News* reported:

"Some people say we're short of talent, but they forget that we won the 1976 NCAA championship with one pure shooter (Scott May)," Knight said. "You just have to find ways to make do."

"I'd say Bob is doing a great job of coaching this year, maybe his best job ever," [Lou] Henson said [coach of nationally ranked Illinois].[7]

Knight is committed to giving books back to the university through his fund-raising activities on behalf of the school's Library Fund. Knight has held three basketball scrimmages a year at cities around the state whereby the proceeds go to the Library Fund. In this way the players are part of the commitment to books and learning. He has solicited hundreds of thousands of dollars, he has prevailed on friends and acquaintances for donations and help, and he has even used the IU student body. Knight's assistance helped the Library Fund obtain a matching grant. Last year there was a donor's list of contributors to the fund in Knight's name two inches thick. The library gave Knight a set of rare Civil War books to show their gratitude for his generous fund-raising efforts.

Knight believes that "basketball should contribute something to the university. What could we do that benefits more people? Everybody uses the library."

In his preseason annual address to the student body, in a packed-full Assembly Hall, Knight announced:

You're a great group. You're good. You're a hell of an example for others. And I want you to have the same pride in your univer-

sity. Now, each of you is going to waste a little money on all kinds
of things this week. I want you when you get home, to take out
your checkbook, and write me a $5 check, made out to the Indiana
University Library. Send it to me at Assembly Hall. We're going
to start a little student fund and I want you people to be the first
to give something to it. It's a great university that you're attending.
You're going to be very, very proud of it 20 or 25 years from now.
But you're going to have to help sustain it. So kick loose $5.[8]

The other part of showing respect for the university is, for Knight,
exemplified by graduation. The degree shows the student appreciates
what a university education is all about.

Bob Hammel is mostly bald, mostly overweight, mostly near-
sighted, mostly rumpled, and mostly Knight's best friend. Hammel
has also been the sports editor of the Bloomington, Indiana, *Herald-
Telephone* since 1966. On the day that he first met Knight in April
1971 (at Knight's press conference to take the basketball coaching
position at Indiana), Hammel asked Knight, "What does the *M* stand
for in Robert M. Knight?" Knight replied, "'Montgomery' but never
print that anywhere." The relationship between Hammel and
Knight grew into one that brothers would have — an indescribable
closeness.

Hammel believes that Knight has a fear that basketball can exploit
a kid, and the one guarantee that it does not is when the student gets
his degree. The program is self-perpetuating in that any potential
recruit to IU knows before he comes what is expected of him academically. "The reputation eliminates a lot of kids."

Hammel feels that "the fact that Jay Edwards is here says he wants
discipline. Edwards could have gone to Louisville (or many other
basketball powers), but the inner man was crying out." Knight really
likes Jay, according to Hammel, but still "chews and rips him in trying
to turn the key in him."

Knight has been extremely successful in graduating Blacks. He
expects them to be good students. There is no easy way out for them.
He treats them as full human beings. Knight believes that "these kids
can't be categorized, but kids are kids. We can't expect the same thing
from everyone on the basketball floor, but we can in the classroom.

Everyone can complete something successfully. There is some curriculum for kids." Coach left the College Coaches Association when he overheard two head coaches talking about their Black athletes learning merely "social graces" at their schools.

Knight is aware of the diverse personalities of his players. He never yelled at Bob Wilkerson and was gentle with Delray Brooks and abusive with Ted Keitchel. When he thinks they can take it, he gets on them.

When any player gets in scholastic difficulty, Knight will enlist the aid of the parents (especially the mothers). In Knight's first conference with Jay Edwards's mother, he was so tough on Jay that Mrs. Edwards didn't want to attend a second conference. Later she went along with Knight's suggestions.

Coach Knight wants the "parents to let us handle their son. We impose restrictions on kids... make kids run stairs at 5:30 in the morning. We never require any kid to do something because of basketball, only academics."

Hammel has seen Knight weep "unabashedly" and deeply over what he has had to do with the kids. For example, in 1978 Knight dismissed three players from the team who lied about smoking marijuana but did not dismiss five others who confessed to using the drug. "Knight asked each player if he had used marijuana. 'Knight made everybody tell everything, with the fear put on him that if you lied you were gone,' the player said."[9] It was Knight's hardest decision in coaching. He felt that he had missed somewhere along the line in getting his message to these players. Knight knew what he had to do; nevertheless, he couldn't control his weeping over this decision in Hammel's presence. Knight's care for his players goes far beyond winning and losing on the basketball floor. His philosophy is tied into the total person, not just the athlete.

Knight has proposed a degree scholarship plan that forces college basketball coaches to aim their players toward graduation. Because of the national embarrassment regarding student-athletes, Knight wants the NCAA to adopt a plan that forces schools to operate without a scholarship for two full years each time one of its athletes ends his four years of eligibility without a diploma. According to Bob Hammel, Knight remarked:

I would give them one extra semester after their four years to get the degree. If they don't get it then, the coach loses that scholarship for two years. . . .

   And that's where the degree requirement comes in. If that kid
doesn't stay in class, he doesn't graduate. And no degree, no
scholarship after him. There's no way a kid can waltz through any
academic institution and get a degree. The faculty has too much
integrity for that. The degree has to be the basis for the whole
scholarship plan.[10]

   The last piece to the academic success of the players is their
success after graduation. Knight discourages his kids from majoring
in physical education (there have only been 5 graduates of the total
48 from the IU basketball team since Knight began his tenure as
coach in 1972).

   Knight admits a strong bias towards business careers. "I try to
   channel all of the players as nearly as possible into some form
   of business because it's very competitive. You're going to get
   knocked on your ass a few times in business just like you do in
   basketball, and you've got to be able to come up and go back.
   I'd be very surprised if a kid played for us and he isn't successful
   in business."[11]

   Of Knight's 43 graduates who used all four years of eligibility, 20
were in business-related majors.
   The success of Knight's players after graduation has much to do
with preparation. The meticulous detail that Knight himself goes
through in game and practice preparation is transferred to his students. Knight has said that the "will to prepare to win is more
important than the will to win."
   Former IU president John Ryan believes that

   no one knows the extent of how Bob has put himself out for the
   kids. He is committed to the idea that the strong must help the
   weak. God made the strong strong. People must also help themselves, but he is sensitive to those who can't help themselves.
   Bob's sensitivity to others forces him to be more demanding of
   the strong and talented—his players.

Knight, however, is not without his critics. Rich Bozich of the *Courier-Journal* (Louisville, Ky.) has questioned Knight's mellowing of his principles. Bozich writes in an editorial:

I grant the man his standards, and I admire him for trying to push college athletics to a higher moral ground.

I only wonder whether his standards are evolving or as bendable as the rims in Assembly Hall. . . .

And hasn't Jay Edwards dribbled right over several principles that even Knight's detractors find admirable in the coach?

Punch the Jay Edwards replay button and you'll discover that the narrow kid from Marion has pushed Knight farther in 15 months than any other IU player managed in 17-plus seasons.

We begin with freshman classroom lapses, jump to $400 in library and parking fines, return to more classroom lapses and move to an unspecified substance-abuse episode that had the coach and player debating how much time Edwards required in a rehabilitation program.

Edwards has hit the Triple Crown of Knight No-Nos. He is also a fearless sophomore shooter who hits strings of three pointers for a team lacking offensive skills.

Coincidence or Compromise?

Has Knight the unyielding grown into Knight the social worker?. . . Knight seemed to resist the notion that he, more than anyone, could inspire behavioral change.[12]

Bozich continues with his explanation of Knight's "new" philosophy concerning Edwards. In November 1988, Knight commented that he would like to see Edwards become a "role model" who would address talks to adolescents about mistakes and what must be learned. Bozich proceeded:

If that's the strategy Knight has embraced with Edwards, it's a wonderful and caring shift in his outlook. I hope it applies to players averaging three points a game as well as 18.2. . . . Has Bob Knight compromised his principles? Or has he simply adopted a broader and more understanding view of Jay Edwards's world?[13]

Several sports writers for the national weekly publication *Sporting News* have agreed with Bozich's criticism. In an editorial entitled "Indiana's 'Deficiencies'" the author asserts that Edwards may not have been treated as harshly as other IU players.

Speculation persists about how much Jay Edwards will play for Indiana this season—if at all. Seldom has one player seemingly held the key to a team's fortunes as Edwards does with this year's Hoosiers.

Cynics have suggested that if Edwards had been the Hoosiers' 10th man, instead of one of the nation's premier guards, he probably would have been run off the team by Coach Bobby Knight....

Addressing several thousand students assembled for his annual question-and-answer session at Indiana, Knight said that Edwards "intrigues me," and called upon his troubled sophomore to become a role model for the state's youth.

"That's what I'd like to see happen more than anything else, and I don't know if he's strong enough," Knight said....

"Off the court, Edwards has been a monumental pain," Knight said. "If Edwards' on-the-floor conduct had rivaled his off-the-court conduct, he'd have been history last year."

Knight told the students that many of them had been guilty of conduct just as bad as Edwards' except that their shortcomings hadn't been publicized.[14]

Another issue of controversy with Knight involves other Big Ten coaches. The cable television station ESPN has an eight-week "Big Monday" doubleheader featuring two Big Ten teams in the second game beginning at 9:38 P.M. eastern standard time (EST). Indiana was slated to play in three of these late-night games, with the likelihood of returning to their home campus at 3:00 A.M. Dave Nightingale for *Sporting News* reported:

"The thing that ticks me off is that we're just doing this for the damned dollars, and they aren't big dollars at that," Indiana Coach Bobby Knight said.

Knight told the assembled media that they could not have access to his players in the locker room after the win over Iowa.

"My kids are going to go home and get some sleep so they can go to class tomorrow," he said.

Knight also had sympathy for the visiting Hawkeyes. "It's simply ridiculous for a team to have to get home at 3:00 A.M. after playing one of these games on the road," he said.

Curiously, this is the same Knight who ordered a 2:00 A.M. workout for his players — in Bloomington — after a 76–65 loss at Illinois on January 28. "Yeah, but that was a Sunday, and the players didn't have class that day," he said.[15]

The other Big Ten coaches need the national exposure for recognition and recruiting. Nightingale's article continues with Iowa coach Tom Davis commenting: "Some of us in this league need to recruit players nationally, and those who do love the ESPN package. It's a tremendous positive."[16]

Besides Knight, there is a second driving force behind the academic success of the Indiana University athletes. "Cut from the same cloth" as Knight, Buzz works toward the same goals with equal zeal.

NOTES

1. Bob Hammel, "Cellist Starker Draws Parallels to IU Basketball," *Herald-Telephone* (Bloomington, Ind.), 21 February 1985, 13.

2. Starker's press release (Bloomington, Ind.) 21 February 1985: 5.

3. Hammel, "Cellist Starker Draws Parallels," 13.

4. Ibid.

5. Joan Mellen, *Bob Knight: His Own Man* (New York: Donald I. Fine, 1988), 15.

6. David England, "Athletics, Academics, and Ethics: An Interview with Bob Knight," *Phi Delta Kappan*, November 1982, 159.

7. Dave Nightingale, "Big Tension in Big 10 Scramble," *Sporting News*, 13 February 1989, 10.

8. Bob Hammel, "A Knight with the Students," *Herald-Telephone*, (Bloomington, Ind.), 29 October 1986.

9. Mike Tackett, "Knight Demanded Facts: 'If You Lied You Were Gone,'" *Chicago Tribune*, 15 December 1978, sec. 5.

10. Bob Hammel, "Knight's Degree-Scholarship Plan Keys Symposium," *Herald-Telephone* (Bloomington, Ind.).

11. John Sherman, "Bobby Knight's Strategy Scores in Business and Basketball," *Indiana Business*, November 1985, 28.

12. Rick Bozich, "Is Knight Mellowing or Bending his Own Rules?" *Courier-Journal* (Louisville, Ky.), 20 December 1988, F1, F3.

13. Ibid., F3.

14. "Indiana's 'Deficiencies,'" *Sporting News*, Editorial, 21 November 1988, 40.

15. Dave Nightingale, "Controversial Late Knight with Hoosiers," *Sporting News*, 13 February 1989, 11.

16. Ibid.

3

Elizabeth "Buzz" Kurpius

Still let us remember how good it was once here, when we were all together united by a good and kind feeling which made us . . . better perhaps than we are.

The Brothers Karamazov

In Assembly Hall five flags hang from the ceiling designating NCAA Basketball Championships — 1940, 1953, 1976, 1981, and 1987. These flags are Indiana red and sway and swagger from the circulation fans. They appear to have a life of their own. The center of the basketball court has a large white outline of the state of Indiana within the center jump circle and contains a large *I*. This 17,357-seat building has been sold out for the last 14 years. The home court advantage has produced 195 wins and just 26 losses since 1972 when Assembly Hall opened. Great players such as Quinn Buckner, Scott May, Isiah Thomas, Steve Alford, and quite a few others have treated these rabid red-sweatered crowds to some of the best college basketball anywhere. The players are often larger-than-life figures to their adoring public. This is a mecca of college basketball.

Buzz's office is less than a good sharp bounce-pass from the Assembly Hall basketball floor. Often before or after practice she'll appear on the courtside and beckon a player or two over for some academic concern. She has their grades before the players receive them. At the end of each semester, there is a steady stream of players coming in to find out their grades in each course. The process is interrupted by assistant basketball coaches wanting to know the grade-point averages of certain players to see if they are eligible. When it is determined that all 14 have made it, a cheer goes up in her office with the four other women that compose the academic support team of Indiana University sports.

Buzz asserts:

I care about the kids. Care that they make it. We have a lot of minority kids. We try to help them find out that they are bright. Mike Woodson was a perfect example.

He was such a poor reader. Everything was a struggle for him. He would go from a game to his tutor. His girlfriend even went with him. What a joy it was to see him and get him to understand that he was bright.

My driving force is to see people succeed in areas where they didn't know they had talent.

Satisfaction is in seeing the kids do well.

Buzz majored in elementary education and recreation, then taught for five years. It is this education background that gave her an understanding of the quest for knowledge that she tries to pass on to student-athletes. Buzz relates a Jay Edwards story about him attending his very first play and enjoying it, saying, "It turned him on."

She still takes classes with the players. In the past year, for example, she's taken jazz and a course on the presidents' wives. She loves books, especially anything by James Michener. This love of learning is a touchstone with new and old players. The walls of Buzz's office are lined with inscribed paintings from former student-athletes — paintings that express devotion and continued friendship.

Buzz has said, "When Coach goes on a rampage, the players come to me. They go through the hard times together, and this solidifies a friendship. The old-timers call to see how things are going. . . . They all stop in."

JAMAL MEEKS

"I'm Jamal Meeks"

Jamal Meeks regularly stops at Buzz's office. He received his first college A this summer in a makeup of course work for which he originally failed. Buzz said, "We literally danced around the office. We were so happy for him. Jamal then got a C on his speech test. He was so depressed because he had studied and he thought that whenever you study you should always get A's in everything."

Jamal is easy to like. He smiles readily and speaks of himself in the third person. Even Coach Knight spoke about Jamal's enthusiasm. Knight said, "He'll [Jamal Meeks] make mistakes, but he will bounce back like a rubber ball. I'm not sure that I've ever coached a kid whose enthusiasm I just simply liked as much as Meeks'."[1]

Jamal speaks with a country accent. One might place him from West Virginia rather than Illinois. He is at ease and at peace with himself. As he recounted his early IU contacts, I wondered what he would be like in three or four "Knight" years:

I was amazed [when I first met Coach] because, I mean, I was. Basketball was important. [Jamal begins to mimic an announcer doing introductions of a starting lineup.] Every young player wanted to play for the best coaches—Dean Smith, John Thompson, Bobby Knight, Denny Crum. Young guys dream of playing for these type of people and when he called me I was like, "Ooh, he called ME. He wants ME to play for HIM." I used to watch Indiana basketball and not pay any attention to it. Like Bobby Knight that the mean man. . . . Bobby Knight called me. I was going crazy, yelling and screaming, "Mom, Bobby Knight called. He wants me to come and see the school." . . . His reputation kind of scared me. I had seen him as being mean. Everybody seen him as being mean. It was like he could do no right. . . . It kind of scared me, but if I go there and he tells me I'm not doing right and I get through that, then I could deal with anything. Anything later in life.

Jamal started off poorly at IU in his freshman year. This pattern really began in his first year of high school. Jamal related those events:

This was kind of a weird situation in high school. My freshman year of high school, I came in, and I was one of the better players as a freshman. . . . I thought since I was one of the better ones, I thought I didn't have to go to class, I didn't have to work. So then

I became ineligible for about two or three games in my freshman
year.... So I had to sit down for two games; it made me realize
that they weren't going to let me play without getting my grades.
So it was kind of weird. They kind of slapped me on the hands.
They showed me I wasn't to be able to play if I didn't do my
work.... I felt like, "How could you do this? I'M JAMAL
MEEKS. I play basketball here. We're winning. How can you do
this? I'm the point guard here." Then they slapped me on the butt
and said you can't play. I realized they were going to keep playing
basketball without me if I don't get my grades.

Even as an entering freshman, Jamal knew the essence of Knight's
system and philosophy. I marveled out loud. "That's great," I said.
"You knew before you got there what he was about. You knew there
was something good behind this madman." Jamal continued to amaze
me with the depth of his understanding of Knight's philosophy.

Jamal felt Knight could read him very well and understand what lay
behind the mask Jamal sometimes wore. Jamal continued, "I could have
the worse day and kind of put my mask on. Yeah, you know one of those
days. He could kind of sort out for me. He'd say, 'Something's wrong. I
could see that on you.' It's weird.... I could see what he was trying to do."

Jamal had his masks just like all of us, and he knew when he was
wearing it. When he first met the IU people, he had facial hair and an
earring and was dressed in blue jeans.

I came in there and kind of looked around at everybody. I had the
crazy haircut and all. [An earring, sneakers, rock concert tee-
shirt.] I went, "Oh, man!" I talked to Knight and he said, "What
do you want to major in?" I said, "Education." He said, "Education is a great thing, but you want a job where you could make
some money. Education is good—I'm not knocking it. You want
something that is going to give you financial stability."... I told
Knight, "I wanted to coach." He said, "That's no problem. I'll give
you your first job here.... You need to get into the business field
where you could make some money." Then he talked about my
classes, my grades in high school, and so forth.... Knight never
said anything about my hair. I guess it was up to the players to
explain it to me, help me adjust, help me along.

I wanted to speak about my profession — education. I couldn't resist the urge to present my argument for a humble but proud career choice. I made a mental note to bring it up later.

When we returned to the summer orientation with Buzz and her staff, I asked Jamal how he felt about the tutors, class attendance policy, and what was academically expected from him. He began:

It was kind of like freshman year of high school all over again. I felt like, "I'm on Indiana's campus to play basketball here. I don't have to go to class. I'm the big man around here. I play for Bobby Knight's team.". . . That's the way I was seeing myself. "I don't have to do this. I don't have to go to class. I don't have to show up for my tutors. I'll just show my face around school."

Then after a while my grades started to slip and Buzz said, "You can't play basketball. If you don't get your grade-point average, you won't play basketball. I don't care what you say or what you try to do. You're not going to play basketball if you don't get these grades." It kind of slapped me in the face. . . . I was like, "There is no way I'll be letting my family down, my friends. There is no way I'm going to fail."

When these events reached Coach Knight's attention, Jamal recalls he was immediately contacted:

That was the day he came in and said, "I'm not going to yell at you." . . . It was right on the court. He pulled me to the side. I sat down on the supports under the basket. He said, "I just want to tell you, you can help this team. You're getting better. If you want to fail, you're hurting us. You're hurting our team. If you just want to think about yourself rather than this team, you fail. If you think about this team, you'll get that grade up." I got the grade up and felt pretty good about it.

Buzz sensed a change occurring in Jamal. She arranged for his tutors and had Jamal in daily to see her. He began to do the things that Buzz and Knight had hoped for.

I started going to see my tutors regularly, maybe two or three times a week. I got my grades up a little better, started coming up a little better.

Now the summer session, I see them [tutors] every day. I had a tutor for eight hours [to prepare for a test]. I have one every day at noon, three, and six-thirty. . . . Probably I see them five hours a day, five days a week.

It seemed to me that Jamal wanted to attribute this turnaround to his own pride.

I don't want to be called in here [Buzz's office] all the time. I don't want Buzz to keep calling me all the time. "Did you see your tutor today? Did you do this? Did you do that?" That's wasting her time, too. . . . I appreciate her checking on me, but I don't want her doing it all the time.

Jamal had a unique relationship with Buzz. She was more than a watchdog monitoring his every move. To him, she was a bit of everything.

At times this could be exasperating for him. He didn't want to be treated like a child. He knew he was bright. I could see the sense of pride in his face. Jamal Meeks, the student. I thought it was a good time to speak about a career as a teacher. He had all the requirements. He was personable, a showman, enthusiastic, and understood himself. He shared those feelings. I told him that he had a nice awareness of himself, that he communicated well, and that we needed more people like him in education. He could be "damn good."

I could see he liked the idea.

Much of Jamal's academic growth could be traced directly to Buzz. I inquired about how Knight influenced him. In reply, Jamal related his first experiences concerning Knight's emotional side.

When you want someone to do something and he doesn't do it, it kind of irritates you. . . . That upsets you. It gets to you. You say it over and over and he still does the opposite. . . . I see why he [Knight] gets mad at some things. . . . Some things he does I don't argue about verbally, but internally I argue.

Jamal understood Knight's frustration but also saw the mistakes Coach made. I asked about his feelings when Knight got upset at practice.

When he got mad at someone you would think, "Okay, let's go. You've got to forget about it. You've got to go forward. You can't go backward." Coach would get mad and say, "Fellows, we're going to do things right. We're not going to make mistakes. We're going to think positive about this. We're not going to think about messing up. Just do it right and we can leave." There were a lot of times I made some silly mistakes, some dumb plays. Coach would correct me.

Jamal knew there was a way to go about your business. He also realized the value of senior and captain Joe Hillman:

Joe was a person who was very good. When I first came here, I didn't like Joe. Then I saw through the year how he was helping everyone. I really liked him. Things Coach was saying was kind of above us. Then he would put it to Joe and Joe would spread it out among us. . . . Some things we didn't understand and we would say to Joe, "Joe, how's this?" He would break it down and show us exactly how it was.

Knight used many teaching techniques. Most good educators know that peer instruction is often successful.

Most fine teachers usually love their students. What was Knight's "love" like?

I see Coach as a person who wants you to do something right and be at your best. I mean, he wants you to come out and play hard every day. I don't care what's wrong. . . . I think he just wants us to be so good, just be the best, period. He wants you to be absolutely perfect.

In spite of what I was hearing from Jamal, the logic was off. Was it his expression of what Knight wanted? Was it the message itself? I was troubled by the "winning being everything" message Todd Jadlow relayed to me. The "perfect" tones found in Jamal's voice also saddened me a bit. I wanted to understand the philosophy, the reasons behind the words.

Jamal Meeks was a "winner" in the best sense of the word. Much of his success goes to Buzz and Knight. Jamal Meeks's success epitomized what had been done for many student-athletes at IU.

By the summer of 1989, Jamal had no facial hair, no earring, and no wild haircut with its two shaved stripes. What remained, however, was "I'm Jamal Meeks." By the summer of 1989, Jamal was a "student."

Buzz hires staff based on five principles: one, be up-front with each other; two, be loyal; three, be task oriented—don't care how many hours it takes; four, be flexible; and five, be your own person.

Buzz and Knight have an excellent working relationship. Of Knight, Buzz says, "His classroom is on the court. Most coaches don't buy into this. They want us to take care of the academics and just take off. Not Knight or his assistants."

Her sentiments echo Knight's:

I just tell them, "You must go to class at IU. Nobody's going to do your work for you. But, if you'll work, we'll provide whatever assistance you need." . . .

I talk to both the students and their parents about being degree-oriented. From the first time I interview a student, we're talking about a degree, and I always tell them when we're planning a program, "Remember, it's not *my* degree program, it's *yours*."[2]

At the 1989 football banquet, Buzz presented eight "football academic turnaround" awards to players who previously had a GPA under 1.50 and then had a turnaround and did well. Head football coach Bill Mallory shook hands with each winner as Buzz read the personal academic story for the delighted academic achievers. As the players were presented with plaques, the crowd composed of family and friends gave them a standing ovation.

One football player approached Buzz after the ceremony and asked to have his photograph taken with her. He wanted to send the picture to his junior high school brother in need of motivation for success in academics.

Later in the program, Buzz, with two of her academic support colleagues, Marge and Anitra, dressed up as IU cheerleaders. Armed with pom-poms and old-fashioned cheers, the trio performed as the crowd roared with delight.

"Two, four, six, eight, who do you appreciate? ACADEMICS! ACADEMICS!"

While Buzz and I were sitting in Buzz's office, the interview was interrupted by the ringing of the phone. I glanced around the office. There were IU sports posters on the walls, signed by the team; Magnus Pelkowski's paintings, and a Wheaties box with Buzz's picture on the cover. The call was from a basketball player. Buzz immediately went into a well-rehearsed dialogue:

Hello, Mark Robinson.

[Pause]

How come you're so hard to get a hold of?

[Pause and laughter]

You told me you were done with girls. I talked to your grandmother yesterday.

[Pause]

Okay. Let me tell you what you need to do and what the problem is. You have to fill out an application for general studies. It is only half-filled out. You don't have a choice. You must get this done.

[Pause]

You have to get a degree first.

[Pause]

You have to be enrolled in a school first.

[Pause]

I want to see bodily that this form is completed.

[A smile on her face and then a pause]

Otherwise you can't get a degree. Do you want a degree?

[Pause]

You need 20 hours in general studies when you come back. I want you to come right here. Will you come to see me? It is imperative that this is taken care of.

[*Pause*]

You could have graduated in May in general studies. . . . You have all the course work done. . . . The important thing, kid, is to get a degree. Are you going to do it my way or your way?

[*Pause*]

YOUR WAY!

[*Laughter*]

A new car!. . . A PORSCHE!

[*Pause*]

That's craziness. Get an old Chevrolet. . . .

She hung up the phone, lamenting, "The Black kids tend not to go into general studies. They feel it labels them as 'dumb.' They all want degrees in arts and science. The only difference is two years of language and one math course."

Writer Mark Nichols visited Buzz to work on a newspaper article purporting the position that IU athletes are taking "less demanding" majors than other students. Nichols implied that athletes do not have either the ability to complete challenging course work or the time. His piece entitled "What Price Glory?: The Demands of Big-Money College Sports Are Forcing Many Student Athletes to Spend More Time Studying Playbooks Than Textbooks" points out that the IU athletes tend to concentrate in business and the "smorgasbord curriculum" of general studies, whereas the general student body is barely represented in this latter area.[3]

Buzz pointed out that a survey of basketball players' majors showed Nichols to be wrong: fifth-year seniors Brian Sloan and Kreigh Smith recently completed degrees in history. Smith is working on a second degree in theater. The four other fifth-year seniors also completed their degrees in subjects ranging from business to fine arts to religion and philosophy. In 1990 seniors Jeff Oliphant and Mark Robinson will graduate: Oliphant in telecommunications and Robinson in criminal justice, both before their eligibility is completed.

Understandably, Buzz is proud of the IU athletes and further highlights their differences. She relates, "They have full-time jobs, so to speak, in athletics, but so do a lot of other students on campus. They all have to make choices around those responsibilities. Isn't learning to deal with that part of the maturation process?"[4]

About the Nichols allegations of softened course work and majors for athletes, Buzz comments:

> People are of the mind that if it's not a medical degree, then how is a student going to get a job? But who's to say that a business degree or a medical degree is better than a degree from SPEA [School of Public and Environmental Affairs] or than one in physical education or general studies?
>
> Society would like universities to be vocational schools. It bases the whole value of a college education on the amount of money returned. I'd much rather see a student choose a degree he or she is comfortable with and interested in, something they'll do well in and have pride in. I think a degree, no matter what it's in, is of great value.[5]

NOTES

1. Scott Strasemeier, "Making an Impact — Meeks Is Causing Trouble for Guards around the Big Ten," *Hoosier Scene*, 27 January 1989, 3.

2. "Classroom Comes First for Student-Athletes," *Indiana '88*, 81.

3. Mark Nichols, "What Price Glory? The Demands of Big Money College Sports Are Forcing Many Student Athletes to Spend More Time Studying Playbooks Than Textbooks," *Indianapolis Star*, F6.

4. "Athletes and Academics," *Alpha Beta — Honorary* 2.2 (March 1989): 1.

5. Ibid.

4

Case Study of Jay Edwards

Love is a teacher; but one must know how to acquire it, for it is hard to acquire, it is dearly bought, it is won slowly by long labour.

The Brothers Karamazov

Up one level from the gym floor of Assembly Hall, then a climb of 50 feet on a ramp, I find the basketball office of Robert M. Knight. In the outer office three secretaries busily monitor phone calls, type replies to letters, and occasionally look up to welcome a guest. The office houses huge trophies, red and white Knight-autographed basketballs strewn about, and piles of checks and mail to sort.

Knight's premise is "that life is hard. You'll need fortitude to live it. Survival is synonymous with successfully competing.... [He is] a realist who teaches adjustment to life as it is."[1] This is where young men come to realize their basketball dreams.

Jay Edwards was sitting under the basket, feet in untied basketball high-tops, propped up on the supports. While his Indiana teammates shot around, as players traditionally do before their daily summer 5:00 P.M. pickup game, he laughed and joked to his former high school teammate Lyndon Jones. Assembly Hall, with all the seats vacant, seemed cavernous, and the ball echoed throughout the gym as it was bounced by one of the group of ten or so lean and spidery athletes. The five-on-five game started without any apparent notification, and Jay Edwards moved fluidly, easily, and effortlessly as he had done hundreds of times previously in countless hours in this state's proudest game. The film *Hoosiers* accurately reflected the passion of Indiana for basketball. Small towns have sold-out gymnasiums that have disproportionately large seating capabilities given their size. Everyone wanted a Jay Edwards to be their hometown hero and lead them to the state championship, as Jay had done three times at Marion High School. He was "Co–Mr. Basketball" in Indiana with teammate Lyndon Jones.

Jay made several high-arching three-point shots that swished through the net, barely causing a ripple of the twine (players call this a "swish" or "all-net" shot). His passes found their mark to an awaiting teammate's hands in full flight through a swirl of legs, arms, and torsos. On defense, Jay shadowed his man everywhere with a graceful looping style. During the Michigan game of Jay's freshman season, he asked the coaches at halftime to let him cover the Wolverines' best player who had destroyed IU in the first half with his scoring. Jay nearly shut him out in the second half, supplying Indiana with an easy win.

Jay's basketball talent was obvious, and the attitude that rankled Coach Knight and his staff and frustrated Buzz Kurpius and her Academic Support Group was just as apparent. Jay was athletically a superstar (the leading scorer as a freshman for IU) and an academic underachiever. He was good but coasting on talent alone. He was bright but barely passing and cutting far too many classes. This was the summer after his freshman season at IU. It had been a troubled year academically for Jay and an up-and-down year athletically for him. Much of his problem stemmed from high school.

Jay had been pampered, coddled, and allowed to float through high school by well-intentioned, but misguided, teachers and coaches. Now he faced Coach Knight and Buzz Kurpius in their and his biggest challenge. Other players had been brought in line over time. Former player Bob Wilkerson (class of 1975) had graduated with Knight's help the summer of 1988 at the age of 35. Knight was constantly on the earlier players to complete their degrees. Even Isiah Thomas (NBA [National Basketball Association] superstar of the Detroit Pistons and multimillionaire) received his diploma in 1988 after leaving IU as a sophomore in 1981. Now Jay was threatening to upset this great tradition of academic success.

Jay was to come in for summer registration after high school graduation but did not show up. Buzz called home and was told by Jay's older brother that his car had broken down. She called again after Jay missed fall registration. Finally getting in touch with Jay's mother (an elderly lady who had Jay late in life, 16 years after Jay's older brother), Buzz told her that Jay could stay home if he was not going to register and come in for orientation and testing. Jay finally arrived, registered, and took the required reading (i.e., Reading Retelling Task) and writing diagnostic tests. The tests showed Jay was very bright but needed some remedial work in reading. Buzz hired a tutor, Terri Keith, to work with him and four other athletes for 2.5 hours a week (1.5 hours of individual computer work was included).

Terri Keith was given the task of working with the most difficult student-athletes. She was in her midforties and had worked for three years as a one-on-one tutor for the Academic Support Group. Terri tutored for three courses: two geology courses (her undergraduate major) and criminal justice. She not only tutored players but taught the freshman adjustment skills necessary for college life (i.e., organizing time, daily schedules, monthly schedules, study habits, and note taking). Terri has three teenage children with learning disabilities. Before tutoring any of her courses, Terri would sit in on the course for a full year, meet the teacher, outline the entire book, and take notes. She often sees herself as a substitute mother for these kids, especially when they need a shoulder to cry on.

Jay was "hard to figure out . . . not responsive." He had a "poker face." You couldn't tell what he was thinking. He did not ask questions but just sat there. He appeared bored. When Terri took Jay to the library to do his research projects, he "would read *Sports Illustrated.*"

After a month, Terri went to Buzz to apprise her of Jay's lack of cooperation. Buzz then went to the assistant coaches, who would go to Coach Knight if the problem warranted his attention. With Jay, it was "up and down" for a month with his work. If he didn't show up for an arranged tutoring session, Jay would have to pay for the session out of his own pocket. Otherwise the Athletic Department paid for all sessions with the tutors.

A conference was called with the Black assistant basketball coach, Joby Wright (who helped recruit Jay and had been in contact over the phone with Mrs. Edwards), Jay, Terri, and Buzz. At this meeting it was explained to Jay what would happen if "he didn't get his act together." Jay promised to cooperate.

It was a promise he would be unable to keep.

Six weeks before Christmas, Terri had had it with Jay. After he lied to her about his efforts to study, Terri became furious and "yelled, and yelled, and yelled at him in the hall" outside the tutoring lounge. Jay "had gone over the line with her." At this point Terri went to Knight's chief assistant coach, Ron Felling, and Ron went to Knight with the information. Terri had consulted with Buzz previously about Jay's attitude. Jay would be benched for six weeks even though he was academically eligible to play. Jay only needed a 1.80 GPA to continue to play; he had a 1.96. Knight benched him even though Jay was the Hoosier's best player. Jay had not shown up for his fall remedial work.

Jay's first-semester freshman classes were picked by Buzz (as was her policy for most athletes). Every freshman was assigned 15 hours (as an insurance policy, with the option to drop down to 12 if necessary; only one eighth of 625 IU athletes drop to 12 credits). Hers was a "plan for success" in the first semester — a sprinkling of interesting courses, courses that counted toward the degree, note-taking and test-taking courses, and courses requiring the reading of books. In the fall semester she didn't pick the hardest courses but ones that would teach useful skills. She wanted the athletes to have four speech courses over their four college years. Buzz felt that the kids should be very articulate because they were so much in the public eye.

Most freshman athletes took "Public Speaking" — S121. The course required two texts and was described as follows:

> This course is designed to help students become effective and articulate communicators and critical consumers of public communication. . . .
>
> *Requirements:*
> 1. Attend all class meetings and participate in class discussions.
> 2. Study the assigned reading. . .
> 3. Take three quizzes. . .
> 4. Give three prepared speeches. . .
> 5. . . . Each student will attend two public speeches and file a critique. . .

There is only one remedial course at Indiana University for athletes, Math 014, and it does not count as credit toward graduation. All other courses that a player takes must be ones that would count toward a degree. This is part of the NCAA's Big Ten normal progress rule.

Hence, Indiana University athletes cannot take remedial courses just to remain eligible. Jay could not take disconnected or easy courses.

Jay was given an Afro-American history course. The professor was Black, Dr. William H. Wiggins, Jr. Wiggins had taught quite a few of the basketball players over his 19 years at IU. Knight had met Wiggins at a basketball banquet and asked him to attend practice (which is normally closed to the outside world) and look in on the players. Knight has extended an open invitation to several professors: Harry Pratter, contracts lawyer; Drew Schwartz, botanist; Robert Byrnes, Soviet history scholar; and Wiggins. This group often went to practice, talked to the players, and reinforced Knight's emphasis on academics first, last, and always.

Wiggins hosts an annual dinner for the players that he and his wife Janice prepare. He has a relationship with the players (especially the Black ones) that extends far beyond the classroom or the basketball court. Ray Tolbert (former IU star player) recently brought his fiancée to meet Wiggins. Wiggins has "looked upon them as our boys."

Wiggins's course A150, "Survey of the Culture of Black Americans," normally had 75 to 110 students. It gave a historical overview of the Black experience in Africa from 1600 through the time of slavery, Reconstruction, and Harlem renaissance to current events. There were two 40-minute lectures and one discussion section of 50 minutes each week. In addition, there was a film every week. The course description was as follows:

This course will explore the origin and continuing evolution of Afro-American culture. . . such as music. . . dance. . . traditional narrative forms. . . customs. . . beliefs. . . heroes. . . food. . . will be studied against a revolving wall of racial oppression. . . with attendant readings: Slavery (Peter H. Wood, *Black Majority*), Jim Crow (Le Roi Jones, *Blues People*), and World War II (John Oliver Killens, *And Then We Heard the Thunder*).

There were five course requirements:

1. Punctual and regular class attendance. . . checked daily.
2. . . . . assigned readings.

3. Periodic written analysis. . .

4. Four (4) objective examinations. . .

5. The completion of up to ten (10) in-class, Wednesday lab assignments.

In addition to the above, the Academic Affairs Office of Buzz Kurpius sent out monthly cards asking the professor to circle the student's present grade estimate (A, B, C, D, or F) and to indicate the probable reasons for any unsatisfactory work:

Two or more absences

Poor attitude

Insufficient daily preparation

Wiggins knew Jay Edwards well since Jay was in his discussion section in class. "The front of his [Jay's] car has a license plate 'SILK.'" When Jay was first brought to campus for his official high school visit, Wiggins was asked to help show Jay and his classmate Lyndon Jones around the campus and also to explain the importance of course work and the academic requirements and work load. "Lyndon was riveted with attention like it was the last words of advice before entering a spaceship. Jay, however, was crinkling a soda can as I spoke."

Wiggins came to know Jay as an "Andy Hardy in technicolor," not a malicious kid but someone "coming of age." Wiggins explained to Jay in private meetings, "What is an Indiana University player? It follows as night to day. If you're admitted, you should graduate." Others hired to support the athletes believed the same philosophy.

Since Buzz came to IU in 1974 as the first "sports only" academic counselor in college history, she has seen many students like Jay Edwards. Her mission was not only to preserve athletic eligibility but, more important, to improve the graduation rate. Jay would prove to be a formidable adversary to IU's excellent record with student-athletes. Nearly 550 Indiana athletes involving 17 sports use the academic support program.

Buzz hires women like herself (i.e., well educated, mature, with teenage children and professional experience) as well as some men. Graduate students are used in some specialty areas, but preference is given to those who most likely will be able to continue tutoring for many years.

When new recruits arrive at Assembly Hall to meet the basketball coaches, they are immediately gathered in Buzz's office. A tentative first-year schedule is discussed, as well as expectations, conference rules, and a student's academic responsibilities. Several forms have to be filled out, which include:

- *Program planning sheet* (duplicate). One for the office, the other for the student. This lists the department, course number, professor, requirements, and credits of each course taken. It must be signed by the student-athlete as well as the academic counselor. This is a tentative list of courses for the coming semester and an alternative list.

- *Practice time sheet* (class schedule). A Monday through Friday schedule (with ten-minute slots), starting with 8:00 A.M. and ending at 6:45 P.M., used to pencil in the week.

- *Personal data and class schedule.* To be filled out each semester by the athlete.

- *Blue and white cards.* Sent one third and two thirds through a semester to each professor asking for up-to-date academic status of the player.

- *Semester schedules — courses taken and projected.* A four- or five-year plan of study.

- *Interview summary.* Adviser form for academic-risk students. It contains course and a week of quizzes, exams, papers, projects, missed classes, tutors seen, and problems.

- *Study table attendance.* Name, time in/time out.

- *Study table recap.* Sent to coach every week for those on mandatory study table.

- *Semester eligibility letter.* Sent to every basketball player at the beginning of each semester with GPA and total credit hours.

- *Quantitative hours.* Sent to recorder of each upper division every spring to verify hours passed toward degree.

- *Financial aid limitations.* Information to monitor permissible aid to athletes.

• *Summer school application forms.*

All IU freshman basketball players must attend a two-day summer testing and orientation program. In addition, these new players must attend, by Knight's decree, a special seven-week noncredit reading and writing correspondence (mail) program before their first semester.

The fall orientation conducted by Buzz is spread over four days. The players are divided into two groups, Groups I and II. On the first day, Group I attends the library session, and Group II attends the orientation session I. On the second day the two groups switch activities. On day three both groups attend orientation session II, and day four is for orientation session IV. Session III is optional.

The library session is conducted at the main library. The players are taken on a brief tour of the library's facilities by a librarian. Then each player is given Handout A, "The Library: Finding What You Need When You Need It," which assigns every student a hypothetical term paper topic. As an example, Handout A for August 15, 1981, contained the following items: putting call numbers in order; floor locations for some call numbers; find three books on your topic and write title, author, and call number of each; find recent issues of six periodicals and choose one article on your topic and list some bibliographic data; and go to microfilm room and locate the *New York Times* copy for the date of your birth—what is the headline?

Orientation session I covers (1) a *time organization exercise* — students have a typical fall class schedule and have to block out the schedule and compute the amount of study and free time; (2) *Figuring GPA exercise* — compute GPA sample and an exercise; (3) *studentathlete responsibilities* — for class (i.e., attendance, exams, inform instructors of expected absences, assignments, etc.), for academic counseling office (i.e., class schedule, illnesses and family deaths, drop or add courses, tutoring, reporting difficulties, make and keep appointments); and for university (i.e., rules and regulations, financial obligations, checklist offenses such as fines, and process forms).

Orientation II deals with (1) tips on doing well, (2) note taking, (3) plagiarism, and (4) questions. Orientation III is a supplemental session involving test-taking pointers for multiple-choice or essay tests. Orientation IV is a small group discussion of a John Underwood article, "The Writing Is On the Wall" from *Sports Illustrated*, May 19, 1980. This article deals with the problems of athletics, academics, and professional sports' myths.

Coach Knight conducts his own "orientation" with the new players. When highly recruited junior college transfer Dean Garret, six feet ten inches, from San Francisco, and his coach, Brad Duggan, first visited Knight, Duggan recalls that the conversation immediately turned to academics:

> We spoke for four hours. Dean's mom was there, Dean's sister, Dean, me and one of my assistants. There was no highlight films, which coaches usually bring, a projector, a screen, films of the most beautiful campus, girls. . . .
> He didn't do that. He just came in and the six of us talked about life, not about basketball. "Where are you going to be in four years?" he asked. "You have to represent your family and yourself outside of basketball. What will you talk about to people outside of basketball?. . . "
> About eighty schools were recruiting him [Dean]; he was the number-one rated community college player in the country. Knight told him, "You will never get any money, you will always go to class or you won't play, you will always act like a gentleman and I will scream and yell at you all the time. But I'll make you as good as you can be."[2]

Magnus Pelkowski, currently a fifth-year player for Knight, had a similar exchange with Coach Knight on their first meeting.

> Within thirty seconds he [Knight] started to talk about academics. He asked me what I was going to major in and so on. Then he said, "Don't miss class. It's part of being disciplined."

Magnus has not cut a class in over four years of study at IU.

> It's your worst nightmare if Coach publically gets on you before practice about cutting. He'll read out loud the teacher's report and embarrass you. Somebody is in deep shit.

The schedule for Jay, besides Afro-American history, contained four other courses. A course in personal health, which covered sex education, drugs, and health education, was among the freshman fall selection. Along with this course Buzz chose a criminal justice course and a first-aid course for Jay. These courses required note taking, tests, and memorization. His fifth course was U190 ("Uralics"—another history course concerning Genghis Khan). Buzz, herself, took the course with the players and found the lecturer very clear and informative. Jay would fail U190 and then repeat it as a summer course with a passing grade of C+.

Because Jay was cutting class, Buzz was notified first by the instructor of the course. Jay was then called in to Buzz's office for her brand of chastisement. If this didn't work, the assistant coaches were notified and would "lean on" the player. Everyone had to attend class.

Assistant coach Dan Dakich played for Knight and was team captain in both the 1984 and the 1985 seasons. He majored in telecommunications as an undergraduate and is currently working toward a master's degree in college student personnel administration. One summer following Dakich's junior year, Dan and five friends signed up for a sociology class. He found the class easy and received a grade of B+ on the first exam. He and his friends decided to take turns attending class, photocopy notes for distribution among the others, and just take the tests. Knight found out about their "master" plan and immediately called Dakich into the office. Was the story of cutting five out of six classes accurate? Yes. Did you get your summer scholarship money? Yes. Pay the scholarship money back in two weeks. We don't give basketball scholarships to people who do not attend class. Dakich scrambled to get a job, earn the several hundred dollars, and repay the money. But in the end he did it. He never cut class again.

Dan was in charge of the "dawn patrol," a punishment for cutting class, which consisted of running five miles or sprinting in the gym at 6:00 A.M. This would normally be the first deterrent for cutting class. Jay became a regular member of the dawn patrol by virtue of his cutting.

There were several other layers before a trip to Knight's office for academic problems was warranted. All players feared the walk up the ramp to his quarters. Knight could take a scholarship away or dismiss someone from the team if he felt it was necessary to ensure academic success.

In the second semester of Jay's freshman year Buzz signed him up for 15 credits: "Black Church and America," "Afro-American Literature," "Introduction to Recreation," "Foundation of Racquet Sports," and "Drug Use in American Society." These courses were mutually agreed upon by Jay and Buzz. In the drug-use course, students spent six to eight hours with high school students explaining and examining the dangers of drugs.

Buzz's philosophy concerning athletes was that you had "to care." She was their friend in the sense that she forced them to do what they had to do to graduate. She was from the "same page as Knight" and complemented his support and power.

At the end of each semester, Buzz reviewed the NCAA and Big Ten Conference requirements to be eligible for competition and/or athletic aid. At the end of the freshman year a student needed at least 24 hours and a 1.80 GPA; after the second year, 51 hours and a 1.90 GPA; the third year, 78 hours and a 2.00 GPA; and the fourth year, 105 hours and a 2.00 GPA. The NCAA requires each athlete to pass an average of 12 hours every semester enrolled. Incompletes were not accepted and counted as an F (failure) on a transcript.

Jay did well in the first part of the second semester because his tutors forced him to do the work. The tutors met Jay during the basketball season in the evening at the Indiana lounge near the academic support office. During summer school Jay had to meet the tutors five days a week, two to three and a half hours a day for the entire six weeks of class.

Buzz kept in contact with Knight through the head manager, Julio Salazer. She sent notes, lists, and memos about Jay and the other basketball players. For example, Jay hadn't registered, he had too many parking tickets, he was cutting class again, he was falling below his current GPA, and so on.

Buzz was angry at Jay and wanted him to know it. He hadn't followed direction or kept his part of the commitment. She was adamant about being on time, and Jay was continually a "no-show." "If [I] lose Jay, it will be his fault," Buzz believed. She had an army of 180 tutors (mostly doctoral students, undergraduates in mathematics or science, or mature women like herself who have families). She was also a surrogate mother to the players. Her office was only several feet from the basketball floor, and Buzz would daily call people over to her to check on their academic progress. All the players had to have calendars. Even the basketball coaches were trained to keep reminding the players to put items on their calendars and constantly check notes.

Marge Belisle is Buzz's academic assistant who supervises the study table and contacts student-athletes on a weekly basis to check academic progress. She was a history and English major in college. She currently tutors the Afro-American course for the athletes. All the incoming players are identified from their SAT scores and high school transcripts for remedial needs. In the first two or three weeks of the fall semester, Marge will get feedback on the progress of the students from their professors. If a problem seems to be developing, Marge will personally call the professor. The office staff have a good relationship with the faculty since most of academic support people are long-time residents of Bloomington. The staff obtain the course syllabus for each course they tutor. The tutors work one-on-one and traditionally have a great rapport with the students.

Marge hires a reading specialist whenever necessary for the players. She starts with an emphasis on note taking by finding someone in class who is a good student and then compares notes with her tutor. Her belief that student-athletes stand out in class and cannot hide is reflected in her tutors stressing "produce work first." All the tutors verbally report the progress of their efforts to Marge. Marge periodically calls parents for all good or bad information. It is at this time that she can uncover any hidden problems at the athlete's home.

Steve Downing, the Black associate athletic director, was also a former IU player for Knight. Knight came to Indiana in 1972 (Downing's senior year). Downing recalls:

> I thought I was doing okay academically with a 2.30 GPA. Coach Knight called me in his office. He had done some research and thought I could do better. I graduated one year later with a 2.90 GPA. He just wanted my commitment in class to be the same as the basketball court.

Downing was himself a number-one draft choice of the Boston Celtics in 1973, and after his professional career was over, Knight insisted that Steve obtain a master's degree. Downing accomplished this feat in counseling from Indiana University—Purdue University at Indianapolis.

Knight asked Downing to come in and work with Edwards since both Steve and Jay had the same high school coach. Jay's mother called Steve to check in on Jay's progress. She wanted Downing to keep an eye on him. She was afraid Jay would play a couple of years, then go hardship and enter the NBA. Downing believed that Jay's mom really loved him but that because she had him late in life, she "let him go" a bit.

After the first semester, Jay received an incomplete in one course and failed another. This gave him a 1.60 GPA instead of the required 1.80 GPA. Knight suspended Jay immediately instead of waiting for the end of the semester. However, by an NCAA technicality, Jay became eligible on the first day of the spring semester (mid-January). But Knight did not reinstate Jay.

Edwards signed up for an intercession independent study — "Self-Instruction in Art" for nonart majors. Jay was competent in art and went to Kurpius's office every day by Knight's decree to do the homework with supervision. In order to get out of his tutoring session at one time, Jay said, "I need to go Christmas shopping." Buzz counteracted this excuse and replied, "Yeah, your mom can pick out a nice shirt." Jay had eight projects to complete in his art course and needed a B + grade to become eligible in the spring. Jay knew that his teammate Magnus Pelkowski with a 3.30 GPA was a successful artist. Magnus was from Bogotá, Columbia, majoring in international business. After the 1987 championship, Magnus drew a poster of Knight, Smart, and the winning last-second shot and sold over 1,000 copies at $10 a piece. With the money he went to Coach Pete Newell's (former University of California head coach) Big Man camp to improve his skills around the basket.

At six feet ten inches and 225 pounds, Magnus is bright and articulate but a marginal basketball player. Jay asked Magnus for help with his art projects. Knight often encouraged the seniors to straighten out the newcomers. "Get the son-of-a-bitch to class" would be a typical Knight exclamation to Magnus concerning Edwards. Magnus found himself doing most of Jay's work. Knight found out about the arrangement and "put a stop to it immediately." Jay would have to do the work alone. He managed to get a B + in the course and was eligible to play again.

Around this time, Jay decided to change tutors and was given 59-year-old Bobbie Robertson (Ph.D. from IU in higher education).

She was employed as a one-on-one tutor for three years. Her course specialties were drugs, criminology, and Uralics (Mongolian and the Genghis Khan era) I and II. She sat in on all the courses for a semester. She would meet Jay twice a week for an hour during the entire semester. Often Jay would "sit and fall asleep," according to Bobbie. Then she would wake him up, yell at him, and finally "bombarded him with questions."

Bobbie had great success with the athletes, especially Keith Smart (the junior college transfer and star player of the 1987 team). Keith was "determined to make it." She met Keith in the summer after his 1988 graduation in a store. Keith said, "Hello, Bobbie. How are you? Haven't seen you in a long time. Thank you very much for all you've done." Suddenly he hugged her tenderly. There in the middle of this store, a Black 22-year-old hugs a White heavyset woman from South Africa while a large crowd of teenagers look on in amazement.

Bobbie was working with Lyndon Jones, Jay's high school, and now college, teammate. She was tutoring him in the athletic lounge in criminology. Lyndon, in fact, tried very hard to overcome his past academic weaknesses:

Bobbie: What century are we talking about?

Lyndon: [*No reply*]

Bobbie: ... talking about the nineteenth century. What was the big shock of Darwin?

Lyndon: [*Hesitates*]

Bobbie: Man comes from —

Lyndon: Ape.

Bobbie: We are looking here at man's development from ape. . . . Now there is the Positive School. What made people become criminals?

Lyndon: [*Doesn't know*]

Bobbie: The three major classes of criminals: [*Lyndon writes in his notebook*] one third of the people are born criminals; some of the people are criminally insane; one half of the people are crimaloids — a sort of reaction. What are the three types?

Lyndon: [*Responds correctly*]

Bobbie: Next we go to Ferr's denial of free will. The major themes are that physical crimes are caused by: climate, race, geographic location, where you were born, anthropological, social effects of population, and free trade.

Lyndon takes notes as Bobbie outlines the material. Bobbie is reviewing from her textbook, which is highlighted, and she also is using course notes from her own notebook.

Bobbie: What is the doctrine of free will?

Lyndon: That's Ferr.

Bobbie: Yes, but what is it?

This continues for over an hour. Repetition, questions, and drill.

The basketball assistant coaches supported the tutors and also reflected Knight's passion for academic success. Ron Felling is Knight's chief assistant coach. He claimed that

Coach demands that the players be the best person that they can be both in the classroom and on the court. He does this with his presence and his approach. He demands that the kids have an insight into where they are going. He wants them to be proud. Coach makes a promise to the players and parents to graduate. He then has a burning desire to push and drive them. When he gives his word toward that goal, he is unyielding. He wants more for the players than they want for themselves. Regarding Jay, Coach talked to him and said, "I'm going to do things for you in your best interest and you may not like it."

Jay would give Coach Knight, Buzz Kurpius, and the support staff plenty of opportunity to do things for him that he may not like. Things did not get better for Jay. In the summer of 1988, Jay Edwards had his car taken away by Coach Knight after an agreement had been reached with Jay's mother. The car, with the license plate "SILK," was replaced with a bicycle. Jay's scholarship was also revoked. Knight would not have any student on scholarship who did not attend class whether it was a conscientious student like Dan Dakich or an outstanding athlete like Jay Edwards.

Knight obtained a job for Edwards at a local brick factory. The work was dirty, hard, and character building. The day began at 6:00 A.M. and went until noon. Then Jay attended summer classes and played basketball at the 5:00 P.M. player-run workout.

At times Knight bumped into Jay Edwards. "What's it like to get up at 5:00 in the morning to go to work? What do your son-of-a-bitching friends think of you now?" Jay had never worked before — not the kind of work that Knight felt would make him or break him. Knight would tell Edwards that he would be playing for the Marion (Jay's hometown) pizzeria in the fall. "They don't televise many games there."

That summer Jay went to work, attended class, and then played basketball at 5:00 P.M. He attended school without a scholarship and passed his courses. Jay said (speaking about Knight), "He said if he didn't want me here, then he never would have recruited me in the first place. He knew I was a good kid. But he wasn't going to sit there and let me not be what I could be."[3] Jay needed help in several ways.

The signs began to add up. Tutors smelled alcohol on Jay's breath. The listless, uncaring behavior could be explained somewhat by the public acknowledgment on September 26, 1988, in the *Sporting News*:

> Indiana's Jay Edwards, the Big Ten Conference freshman of the year last season, is lost for the 1988–89 season and is slated to enter a chemical abuse program.
>
> The 6-4 guard, who averaged 23.3 points in the Hoosiers' last 12 games last season, has been embroiled in controversy during most of the past year. He was suspended last December for five games by Coach Bobby Knight for academic difficulties and lost his scholarship last July because of more academic uncertainties and several hundred dollars in unpaid parking and library fines. . . .
>
> [Edwards]". . . I'm just going to tell Coach how I feel, and if he can't handle that I guess I'll just have to go about my own business the rest of the semester and finish school here and see where I can go. I'm doing well in my classes, and I don't want to drop out and start my life almost over."[4]

Felling and Knight agonized over what to do with Jay. Felling recalls:

The string had run out. Now the ball was in the player's court. Whether Jay shoots another basket for Indiana is unimportant. Coach Knight aims for goals higher than ten feet. Coach abhors drugs. He is extremely disappointed. He has said in speeches to "take drugs and stick them up their asses."

Ron believes that "come bleed or blister" the players will get Knight's message. Knight stayed with Jay and supported him at his lowest moment.

NOTES

1. Joan Mellen, *Bob Knight: His Own Man* (New York: Donald I. Fine, 1988), 283.
2. Ibid., 155.
3. Ibid., 283.
4. Stan Sutton, "Drugs Bench Indiana's Jay Edwards," *Sporting News*, 26 September 1988, p. 51.

Bob Knight
Basketball Coach

Ralph Floyd
Athletic Director

Elizabeth Kurpius
Associate Athletic Director,
    Academic Affairs

Marge Belisle
Academic Counselor

Photos courtesy of Indiana University

Anita House

Steve Downing
Associate Athletic Director,
    Regional Campus & High School
    Coordinator

Mary Rose

Photos courtesy of Indiana University

Matt Nover

Joe Hillman

Eric Anderson

Jamal Meeks

Todd Jadlow

Bob Knight

Photo courtesy of Indiana University

Bob Knight

Photo courtesy of Indiana University

Joe Hillman

Photo courtesy of Indiana University

Eric Anderson

Photo courtesy of Indiana University

Jamal Meeks

Photo courtesy of Indiana University

Todd Jadlow

Photo courtesy of Indiana University

The Indiana trophy case

During a practice session, Knight will position himself under the basketball supports

Photos courtesy of the author

The NCAA Championship Banners in Assembly Hall

Outline of the state of Indiana at center court

Photos courtesy of the author

5

Hard-Love

For love in action is a harsh and dreadful thing. . . . Active love is labour and fortitude.

The Brothers Karamazov

Players filed out of the locker room. Some were dribbling balls. Others appeared with high-top sneakers, laces untied, and sat down on the wooden bench to fasten them. A few stretched out on the gym floor of Assembly Hall and began to twist and contort. Eventually the eight baskets were rattling with jump shots and dunks throughout the ten minutes of "prepractice." The mood was light? Uneasy? Serious?

Diagonally across the floor from where the players entered, Knight emerged from his corner locker room. He walked determinedly and purposefully, with head down, to center court. All the basketballs were immediately dropped to the floor, and the players, in quiet procession, went back into their locker room, followed by Knight. It was a strange ritual, like the moon coming up in a horror flick and the zombielike creatures methodically proceeding to their macabre tasks.

The "chalk" session involved the offense of tomorrow's opponent (Kentucky), defense, and individual matchups. Reemerging back onto the court after the 15-minute mental refreshing, the players now could begin practice with the knowledge that they had every possible bit of information concerning tomorrow's opponent. The five-on-five part of practice began with the Indiana University second team running Kentucky's offense against Indiana's starters playing defense. Knight took his customary seated position under the basketball standards while the assistant coaches conducted this phase of preparation.

"Jadlow, what the hell are you doing?" Knight bellowed. Knight quickly got to his feet to move toward the mistake-prone Jadlow. Everyone froze. Jadlow slouched on one leg, and the six-feet-nine-inch senior looked to the floor with a stoic face a poker player would envy. Jadlow was the starting center after being a part-time performer for most of the previous two IU seasons. Jadlow was this year's "whipping boy." "For three years we've been trying to teach you how to step out on these screens. We can't win if you don't help in these situations," Knight continued. It was a five-minute explosion by Knight in which all that Jadlow had been, is, and will be was brought into question by Knight. Jadlow, with head tilted toward his feet and one arm resting on his waist, listened without acknowledgment and held that deadpan expression on his face. The other players acted as if they were caught eavesdropping on a telephone call. They looked anywhere but at Knight, who was now face-to-face with Jadlow.

Knight made his point and started to walk back to his floor seat when suddenly he whirled back toward the recently maligned Jadlow. This aftershock from Knight was more terrible and devastating than the first. The players still had not moved from their original frozen positions, having sensed that the Jadlow blistering was not quite over. "Jadlow, you'll sit on the bench next to me for the rest of the season," Knight began again. "You've never understood after three years what we are trying to do here." And on it went for all the onlookers for what seemed like an excruciating long time.

Realizing that it was not actually Jadlow that Knight was railing on and on against, the players knew it was each and every one of them. It was them, their values, their generation, and their work ethic.

Father Zossima, in Dostoevsky's *The Brothers Karamazov*, described a kind of "hard love," and Knight treated his players with the same peculiar affection. A love so deep that at times Knight had to grab them by their jerseys and shake them, at times weep openly over them, at times question their manhood, and at times hug them. His love was powerful, demanding, and often difficult to accept. He cared so much for them that he corrected their mistakes, told them no, scolded them, and made basketball practice as hard as possible on them so that "life after Knight" might be just a little easier.

TODD JADLOW

"It Really Didn't Bother Me at All"

The road has only two lanes. I have difficulty getting around first one pickup truck, then another. The drivers look at me peculiarly as I pass them. At one time I am stopped by a tar-spreading crew. A man holding a red "STOP" sign and a green "GO" on the other side eyes me warily. I smile and he returns the gesture. A mouth opens and reveals a few lonely teeth. It is difficult to tell whether he is 40 or 60. I can smell the tar and see the heat rising from the road in misty clouds. The smells take me back to a tiny Ohio country town when I was a boy.

Fidgeting with the radio I can mostly get country and western music, but the National Public Radio station I desire keeps fading away from me. The GO sign is pivoted toward me. I nod and continue my journey. Eventually I find Greenfield, Indiana, the summer residence of Todd Jadlow.

The house is easy to find since there are but a few blocks in the hamlet. Todd must be the biggest person in the history of tiny Greenfield. I am greeted at the door by Todd and notice a young boy watching television intensely. The videotape *Willow* is playing with the featured character played by a dwarf. Todd seems, to me, at six feet nine inches and 230 pounds, disproportionately out of place here.

Todd graduated from IU's School of Public and Environmental Affairs and had been taking graduate courses in the same area while finishing his basketball eligibility in five years at IU.

I expect to find a tortured soul. Someone that Knight has dehumanized and broken—as the critical press would make one believe. What terrible secrets lie inside this sad giant? What difficulties had he faced? I start to question slowly, slyly, and determinedly to my tragedy-seeking ends. I begin by asking Jadlow about his prep-school experience and early contacts with the Indiana staff.

In high school I went to a private Catholic school and pretty much a requirement to maintain good grades. You were looked down upon if you didn't. I went to private school in grade school. Everyone took pride in what they did. . . . It was real strict through junior high. . . . I eased back a little bit in high school. . . . In

Kansas, athletics aren't as big as they are here. You weren't given anything special because you were an athlete.

Jadlow had many offers from Division I schools. He wanted to attend a high Division I school. He continues:

The offers were from mid-Division I's. Arkansas State and New Orleans. My main intention was to go to the University of Kansas; so I talked to Coach Brown a couple of times and he said I could have a scholarship but there were six incoming freshmen and there was no way I was going to play, so I decided to go to junior college for a year, get some playing strength, then transfer to Kansas.

Jadlow enrolled at Barton County Community College, where he maintained a 4.0 grade-point average. Once there, the Indiana staff contacted him through one of the assistant coaches. Jadlow describes his first contact with Knight:

Kind of in awe a little bit. I had never watched Indiana basketball before or even much college basketball until now. I knew he was a team coach. I was really impressed with what he had to say. I didn't know anything about him except that he was one good coach. He stressed that academics are an important part of Indiana basketball. To succeed on the court you have to do well in the classroom first.

After a few more background questions, I sensed that he wanted to get to his story. Was the player that Knight was the hardest on always a senior?

I think that Coach got on them [seniors] and channeled everything through them. In my first year it was Winston Morgan, a senior; then the following year, senior Daryl Thomas; the next year, senior Steve Eyl. Then my turn.
  I think he expects a lot from seniors. He expects them to show the underclassmen.

It was clear that mistakes made by seniors were not to be tolerated by Knight.

> He expects the seniors to think like him—to know what he wants done. If you don't do that, he'll tell you how it's going to be done. Coming here there is a lot of learning. I've been here four years, and I still have so much to learn from Coach Knight's system.

Todd enjoyed his redshirt year (owing to an ankle surgery) because it was a pressure-free learning experience.

> It was the funnest year I ever had. You're really learning everything and having a fun time. There is absolutely no pressure put on you whatsoever. You're just out there playing, having fun. When the team goes away, you stay in Assembly Hall and work. You don't make the road trips.

I couldn't wait any longer to get to Todd's senior-year experiences with Knight. I shifted forward in my seat at the kitchen table, paused, and tried to peer beyond Todd's eyes as deep as possible.

> It really didn't bother me at all. I think when you start to think about it and really think about what you did wrong and what he's trying to say, it probably gets to you the most. You just try to let it blow over and it will be okay. . . . Anything and everything was said. Anything he said you can't take personal at all because he's trying to make you a better player, and at the same time he's trying to get you to play harder. . . . When he says to me, when he's getting upset, people ask me after a game, "What did Coach Knight say to you?" and I can't even tell them. I really can't. I don't even—I shouldn't say I don't pay attention, but you try and listen to the good things he says and not everything else.

Jadlow then discussed *what* was happening during the episodes with Knight. It was not what I expected. I did not want to believe his explanation.

I had been there three years. I knew what was going on. I knew that he was trying to get everyone else playing by channeling a lot of things through me. . . . I think he knew that I could handle it. It didn't really bother me at all. The only thing that ever bothers a person are more or less the mind games where you can't figure out what you did or why it's gone wrong. Coach never really bothered me whatsoever. I have to admit a couple of times it got to me. Just like anything, you are going to have goods and bads and you have to take them for what they are. . . . It was something I was told when I first came here: "Listen to what he has to say." I don't show much expression when he yells at me anyway. Yeah, it's like okay. It's like "Are we done?"

I wondered if Todd ever challenged Knight at these moments. Had he stood up to Knight? Did he retaliate? Tell him, "Go to hell!"?

Oh no, no. I put in too much time and hard work to do something like that. That's one thing you know. You work really hard while you're here. You try to keep everything in perspective with all that's going on. It would be really stupid to say something back and jeopardize all the hard work you've put in.

My next thoughts were that Knight and Jadlow must have met before the season at which time Knight would outline his treatment of the senior. Did Knight come to Jadlow and explain his motives? How was it that Jadlow understood what was happening so clearly?

It happened quite frequently that he would have me in the office. Practice would be over and he'd call me in to speak to me. He really did try and communicate with the players. . . . It was personal—like talking to your father. It was about trying to get an understanding of what he wanted done. . . . I knew what was expected of me and when I didn't perform to the expectations, I knew what I had coming. I think this relationship with us is very well. I have nothing but great praise and thoughts for him. It doesn't matter what happened or what people say. . . . It's like a family, you know: If someone gets out of line, you're not punished but reprimanded.

What about his love? It was something I needed to know. Did Todd feel, see, or understand the hard-love?

> It's really a strict system here, and a lot is expected of you. He really cares for all the players. I mean, he does a lot of things for us. . . . He puts in a lot of hard work and everyone on the team appreciates it. . . . If everyone on the team has the work ethic that he has, the team could never be beaten. He puts in endless hours.

Todd's voice remained deadpan and unflinching. I thought this was how he was with Knight, his mentor, teacher, and coach. There were no ill feelings, no animosity between the two — just a working relationship.

I tried to detect a hidden message in those eyes — a look or something that would tell me more, but there was no betrayal of his words. The horror stories — the vengeance — Todd was as incapable of deceiving me as he was incapable of hating Knight. He knew that it was the loving father that corrects the errant son.

Only once in the interview did he even mildly raise his voice. It happened when I asked if this remarkable past season had been, as so many sports authorities had chronicled, "Knight's greatest coaching season" because it was accomplished with average-to-mediocre talent. Todd was upset at this notion because it reflected directly on him.

> It wasn't his greatest coaching year. It was his Olympic team with all the great awesome talent and putting that team together. We were a team just like any other team. It was like Coach always said, "No one thinks we have talent on this team and they are so wrong. We got a lot of good players or obviously you wouldn't be at Indiana."
>
> Our team plays real well. We try and play smart. The key to any basketball game is playing smarter than the other team. It doesn't matter what the talent is. . . . I think the mental approach that everyone adapted from Coach was beneficial. . . . He'll take quotes from Napoleon or Winston Churchill and connect them into basketball.

I tried one last time to see if he harbored any ill feeling toward Knight. I had to satisfy myself, to probe one more time. I studied that face. The same face on which Knight had also been unable to see emotion. No fear, no hatred.

There is certainly times that you get quite upset. At times I'm really angry about what is going on and other times I'm extremely happy. You just have to find a balance. Things aren't going to be great all the time. Just like in the business world, you can have your good days and bad days. That's the way it is here.

The message I kept getting from Jadlow was that it was like a "family" at Indiana with a caring father. The players were there for each other. Knight forced them to rely on each other. To try to buttress each other against the time that Knight would be "on them." Knight had created a strong unit by his premeditated diatribes.

Everyone on the team is very supportive. If anything bad ever happened, everyone came up to you after practice or during practice and would say, "Don't worry about it; everything's okay." Just like this year I even had guys on the team calling me at night asking, "Are you okay? A rough day." Everyone supports each other. There wasn't a lot of bitching.... Everyone seemed so close. We respected each other.... Everything that's instilled in you at Indiana through Coach Knight and the whole system you carry on to your life. All I'm concerned about is winning, being a success, doing what I feel is right while doing the best I can.

I finally asked this gentle young man to describe the man who has had such a strong impact on his life.

Coach is a combination of everything. Teacher, coach, father figure.... A role model for basketball players.... Tough-minded. ... You would like to think you are a better person from being around him. You can handle any problem that comes up. You take a lot from the program with you. Success is what you make it. If you take from here what's been taught to you, you'll be a success.

Todd is going to the NBA tryout camps. He will probably get cut since slow White players do not have a big market in the "run-and-gun" professional leagues. Perhaps he'll end up in Europe playing in a lesser league but extending his career and making a very good salary. Todd will still be getting screams, encouraging teammates, and continuing to play with that expressionless face that hides so much reflection.

JOE HILLMAN

"The MVP"

Knight draped one arm around the six-feet-two IU captain, Joe Hillman. Hillman had arrived at IU from California high school stardom without a scholarship. Clearly he was Knight's "favorite." With his free arm, Knight gyrated in exact floor directions, emphatically demonstrating the proper angles of execution. Joe's responsibility as captain was to make the team understand what had to be done, then to get them to do it.

Hillman was Knight's Most Valuable Player (MVP) during the 1988–89 season in spite of Jay Edwards's game-winning baskets and All-American status. In Hillman, Knight found someone who served as the buffer between the mentor, taskmaster, and players who "did not know what was good for them" or at least could not understand what they needed to know. Joe culled the message from Knight's rantings. He stabilized shaky egos and injured feelings.

"Get those bastards to set down screens and pop out, Joe, or we can't get Edwards open. We'll never get a shot off." Knight's voice rose so that all could hear the private conversation.

Hillman had earned only one B since the seventh grade and had already acquired a business degree at IU as well as been honored as an Academic All–Big Ten selection. He, like Jadlow, took graduate-level courses in his fifth year. Joe was physically smaller and slower than most college athletes. Knight, however, had given him the honorable and most difficult assignment of guarding the opposing team's best player. The running of the Hoosier's intricate offense with its constant screening and cut was also entrusted to Joe.

When play resumed, Joe, like a first sergeant, shouted out orders and directions. He made certain plays were run to completion with the exactness and precision that Knight demanded. The players responded to Joe with the incident of Jadlow fresh in their minds. Practice went crisply and without incident for the remainder of time the team worked.

"I'm one of the guys who has been around here the longest. I've played more than anybody else has," Hillman said. "I feel that I am the kind of guy who knows what Coach wants. So, I've got to make sure that everybody understands that."[1]

Joe realized that he was ordained by Knight to fill the leadership role left vacant by the graduation of star player Steve Alford. Each year Knight selects a player, usually a senior, to serve as a buffer, an interpreter of Knight's words and actions, and to be a "Knight" on the floor.

I asked Joe about leadership and also Jadlow, the designated senior to incur Knight's wrath.

[Steve] Alford took more shit than anybody else from Coach. There is no "whipping boy" here. It is just Coach's way of getting guys to play. There is a lot of learning and teaching with Knight. The older players have been told things, and they shouldn't have to be told twice. Knight might call me on the side and say, "Let's make sure that it gets done."

I was corrected about any notion of the amount of yelling Knight does. Joe was extremely confident, as one would expect the Indiana captain to be, when he replied:

It is a misconception how much Coach yells and screams. Anybody that has attended practices regularly knows how much he compliments and how little he yells.

My mind wondered, Is this Captain Joe talking or Knight himself? Then Joe commented on the players' relationship with Knight to confuse my previously held conceptions further:

He liked our team a lot and was awfully patient with us. We, however, had a long way to go. . . . Our only contact with him is at practice and the games. There is no other relationship. This bothers him a little bit, but a lot of people are intimidated by him. Part of his success is that he has got to keep that distance. We've got to listen and to respect him. Everybody is in awe of what he knows.

At this moment I felt sorry for Knight and the players. They really had much to offer each other, but their roles prevented them from attaining more personal growth. The players could teach and learn as well as Knight. Knight has much to give, but channels are, perhaps improperly, obstructed. Knight chose Joe as his captain in the 1988–89 season and later named him the MVP of the team, much to the chagrin of leading scorer Jay Edwards. Because of Hillman's play in the 1987 NCAA championship game won by Indiana, Knight stressed Joe's experience to his current teammates, saying:

Hillman made six assists and didn't turn the ball over once in the final [championship] game and played on a national championship team. . . . There isn't one SOB in here that's ever done anything like that so let's pay attention to what the hell he is doing. . . . Watch Hillman and see how he plays and pattern your play after him. . . . He's just a good, tough, smart kid.

And the great thing about Hillman is, if you were to ask what kind of basketball player are you, he would start out by saying, "I am a very, very average athlete and there are some things that I have to do that athletes don't have to do." He has a great understanding of what he has to do to play, maybe as good as any kid I've had.[2]

Joe is presently playing outfield and first base for the Class A Modesto minor league team. His hitting is not what he would like, but the Oakland A's feel that he is a good prospect. Joe did not have to return to IU for his final year of basketball. His mother did not want him to. Joe said he would and explained the situation:

Everyone was supporting us when it looked like the season was going to be long and heartbreaking, but you could tell they probably felt more sorry for us than anything. I guess to put it the best way, when I was deciding if I was going to come back for a fifth year, my mom said, "Oh gosh, why? You're not going to be a very good team, and being a senior, you're going to have to take most of the pressure and blame."

I just told her and myself, let's just see. You never know what's going to happen.[3]

There was another problem in his returning for his final season. Joe had a baseball invitation to play in the Arizona Instructional League, which concluded their season in late October. He would thereby miss the first month of classes at IU. Joe got hold of Coach Knight with his dilemma.

"I called Coach Knight and told him I was going to the instructional league, and that it wasn't going to be over until November," said Hillman. "He told me he was going to try to work it out for me to come back if I wanted to. I said, 'Yeah, I'd love to come back and play.'"[4]

Knight contacted Buzz Kurpius, who enrolled Joe in correspondence courses until he would return to IU and then take eight-week courses. Buzz sent Joe textbooks and syllabi, and Joe called his professors to get assignments.

Knight summed up Joe's decision by commenting, "Who wouldn't want to come back for a fifth year for a nice guy like me?"[5] Knight's humor is not well known outside his close associates and players.

Joe knew that Coach needed him and never regretted his decision to finish his final year of eligibility.

Again, Knight had motivated, manipulated, or coerced his troops to another excellent practice. This was and is part of his genius. Few coaches are able to get their players "up" for every practice. He has the ability to make people overachieve, to prepare meticulously, and to go about their business with a certain confidence that they are doing something properly. Today it was the upbraiding of player Jadlow, followed by the surrogate authority bestowed on Hillman tact.

Indiana had not beaten Kentucky at Lexington in 60 years, but with this team of small overachievers, IU would crunch the Wildcats in their own arena 75–52.

Even the Kentucky players were generous in their praise of the defense designed by Coach Knight. Sean Sutton, Kentucky point guard and son of Kentucky coach Eddie Sutton, pinpointed the reason for Indiana's surprisingly easy victory:

> Coach Knight is just such a good coach. . . . I knew he'd have his team very well set up and ready to play us tonight.
>
> I love playing for my father but, as I've said before, my second choice would certainly be coach Knight. If I couldn't play for Dad, I'd love to play for coach Knight. . . .
>
> They just did a great job. No doubt it was the best defense we've played against this year. Their team is so smart and they work at it.[6]

It's been said of Knight that if he has time to prepare, his team will beat any. Similarly, given time, his student-athletes tend to be successful.

I heard the voices of the seniors testifying to their personal experiences and growth, but how did the process affect the freshmen?

ERIC ANDERSON AND MATT NOVER

"I'm Glad I'm Not Him"

These two youngsters share an apartment on Jackson Street just a mile or so from Assembly Hall. The complex comes equipped with an outdoor half-court, which was currently being used for a three-on-three basketball game. The backboard had a red on white sign painted: IU National Champions 1987. These athletes, toiling on a high-humidity, high-temperature day, are certainly aware of the Hoosier's basketball traditions and also of their two well-known apartment neighbors.

As I approached Apartment D (with the *D* missing), a young coed passed me and said, "They're waiting for you. It's the door on the right without a letter. Matt's been coming out every five minutes to look for you." Inside, the apartment had a large Indiana map hanging on the wall and another gigantic (ten feet by two feet) printed poster with an IU basketball saying. There were a couple of pairs of high-cut sneakers strewn on the floor. Even though I saw them I still managed to stumble

over them. Throughout the well-lived-in rooms, two clean and cheery
young men sat down with me. Matt is handsome despite a curve in his
nose from some basketball war or other. His face always kept a slight
smile ready to break into a bigger one on a moment's notice. Eric is a
bit shyer and turned red when the attention was directed toward him.

I inquired about their academic backgrounds and how it was they
came to Indiana. Eric began:

> I had honors courses and calculus. . . all the advanced placements
> in high school. . . . Knight first contacted me in my sophomore
> year and mostly stressed academics as a big part in recruiting me.

Eric won the "Mr. Basketball" title in Illinois, which went to the state's
best player. He also won All-State, McDonald's, Parade, and Converse
All-American honors in high school. Historically Indiana University
had *not* gotten the best athletes in the country. Eric would be an
exception.

Eric related that Knight's pitch in recruiting him was especially effective since he had always had someone to watch over him academically.

> A big part in recruiting me was the academics. At Indiana he
> makes sure that you go to class, and I was always, in my way,
> lackadaisical. I always had a mother who would make me do my
> homework. I just knew if I went to a place that didn't make me do
> it, I would slack off. I was that type of person. I needed someone
> to coax me. . . . Knight's reputation is really why I wanted to go
> here. Everybody says, "You can't play for him. You shouldn't go
> there." Whenever somebody tells you that you can't do some-
> thing, well, I want to do that. . . . It kind of made me want to go to
> Indiana even more. . . . I wanted to prove I could play for him.

Matt had been an excellent high school student as well. In his first
season at IU he would be red-shirted. He could practice with the team
but not play in games or go on the road trips. Coach Knight suggested
that Matt develop physically and needed to learn the system a bit better
before he could contribute. Matt's background was not athletically as
outstanding as Eric's, but academically Matt was an exceptional student. He began to relate the events that led to his arrival at IU:

He [Knight] said his record for graduating people was very high. "You're going to come up and graduate.... We wouldn't recruit you if we couldn't use you."

I wondered if there were a "Knight" standard of academics rather than an IU or NCAA eligibility standard. Eric interrupted and rushed to relate his most recent meeting with Knight:

He's expecting a lot better things from me than somebody who didn't do as well in high school.... He called me in last week in his office and told me, "This is bullshit. You should be doing a hell of a lot better."... He expects more out of me.... He said it to me and I have to do better. I respect him a lot. If he feels that I could do better than I know, then I know that I probably would do better.... I would feel like I'm letting him down if I don't do well.

Eric then spoke about Knight's actions. "Everything he does is for a purpose.... Everything he does, even if it seems a little crazy, there's something behind it.... He might do it a little different... but that's the way he gets his message across and it's done effectively." I asked for an example. Eric went to Jadlow:

Jadlow was pretty much the big man that he picked on this year. He would get really mad at him for us. So that we would know not to slack off. I guess it's his way... Jadlow was always getting pulled off to the side. He was the guy who was a senior.... When you're a senior and an important part to the team and things aren't going well, he goes right to the senior.

Why did he use Jadlow in this role rather than the other seniors— Kreigh Smith or Brian Sloan? Eric commented:

Brian worked hard and got the most of his ability. Knight liked what Brian was doing. Kreigh... he had just given up on Kreigh. Kreigh would just mess around in practice. He [Knight] gets to a point that if you're not going to put out, he's just going to forget about you. And when he is yelling at you, it means he does care about you. When he leaves you alone, it's the time to worry.

So Kreigh was discarded — the ultimate punishment. He was left alone. When I first came to Bloomington, Kreigh was the first to make eye contact with me and pass along a welcome smile and hello. The others, at first, seemed like they did not notice me moving about, taking notes.

I was curious about how the freshmen go through the academic and athletic processes. What if they get benched for a few games in a row? What if they become the next "Jadlow" with regard to the criticism? Eric was a starter and a star player as a freshman. What if Eric could not play for a time?

> I know it could happen. I've been thinking about it. Next year I'll be one of the most experienced guys on the team. If things are going bad, I'll be the one that he'll come to. . . . I've been thinking about it. . . . I know it's more than likely going to happen. . . . He's going to get mad at me and not play me. I just have to get through it. It takes a lot to get through it. You really have to be tough. . . . When a player is not playing, it's the worst thing you can do to a player.

I knew that I had struck a chord in Eric. He did not want to think about the inevitable, but he knew he had to. He blushed and became a little flustered. The subject bothered him. I felt bad for him and remembered to myself how the 1987 star of the championship game, Keith Smart, had fallen from the top of the college basketball world as a junior starter. During Keith's senior year, for about a month he did not move from the bench. It was incredible. From superstar to bench warmer. Eric probably knew the story and more stories than I did.

I quickly turned to Matt and asked him, "After sitting out for a year, what would happen if you did not play next year?" He replied, "That's something even right now I don't want to think about. My heart won't let it happen. . . . I know what's going on. I'm ready to accept the big challenge. I'm going to do all I can."

Even Matt did not want to go into this. He would fight off the new freshman recruits coming in with their press clippings. He had a year of experience and the mental toughness it would take to accept the challenge. I decided to switch back to the Jadlow-Hillman roles.

Matt felt that Joe was very helpful, especially at first. Hillman would yell at the players, a role that Coach expected. Eric and Joe sat next to each other in the locker room and benefited from that close proximity. Eric described this relationship with Joe:

At half-time he was always giving me a whack on the leg and telling me to play. Joe could hit pretty hard. [Eric laughed.] It would wake me up. He helped me a lot. He knew he was going to take the blame if we lost. Joe's the guy who would be responsible. "Joe, why don't you get these guys playing?"—that's what Coach would say. "You're better than this. It's your fault." . . . Joe would be the guy to get us out of it. It helped us out a lot.

Again I pursued the Jadlow experiences at practice. How did the two youngsters feel as they viewed this? Matt began:

At the time I was thinking, "I'm glad I'm not him." I hope I never get to be in that situation where he explodes on me. That's kind of what he wants you to think: "Don't mess up like Todd. He did something wrong; he's getting in trouble for that."

Eric had another perspective:

Todd's a senior. He should know better. He's been in the system for four years. . . . Knight would say in practice, "You fifth-year seniors have been here for five years and you're still making the same mistakes." What he means is that if you're making the same mistakes after five years, it is unacceptable. . . . I was a freshman and making the same mistakes, but he wouldn't get as riled up at me. . . . I think Todd got the most out of what he had. I can't see him doing more with his physical ability.

I asked Eric what it was that he personally felt as Todd was being berated by Knight.

I felt sorry for him. Nobody likes to have somebody in your face. . . . There's not much you can do. He would get down. He would isolate himself from the team. You couldn't talk to him.

Do you wonder if you made the right choice in coming to Indiana University? Eric began:

> I tell you that there are some crazy things about it, but the benefits are so great. Just playing at Indiana. I think it's the greatest place in the world to play basketball. The fans just love basketball so much. I wouldn't give it up for anything. Just playing at Assembly Hall. . . . We win. It's just the greatest feeling to win. . . . No one knew how we won games. We just did what Coach said and we won. I think this year is the greatest example for me and the guys coming in — all you have to do is do what Coach says and you'll win. . . . That kind of makes it so much sweeter. The way we win is so incredible.

That was a special attraction for these kids to come to IU. Beyond Knight, there was the basketball mania of this state, which made these young men larger-than-life figures. Figures to be praised, to be scrutinized, to be studied, to be analyzed, and to be hailed as saviors.

Finally I asked them about Knight's special brand of love. I had placed the idea in their minds in our earlier phone conversation. I wanted it to simmer so that their response was rich. Eric responded beautifully:

> I think he's hard on us because it's so apparent that he really loves his players to the fullest. . . . When you go through four years with him and you're out, he does all he can to get you a job; he looks out for us. He's loyal to whoever he had in his program. He does all he can to let you be a better player. A good example of this is Chuckie White, who left a month ago. He [Knight] was really puzzled and really felt bad that he had recruited Chuckie. This really wasn't the place for Chuckie to excel. I was talking to Coach about Chuckie. He really feels bad that he recruited Chuckie here. . . . He wanted to know what he did wrong. Everything he does is to help you be a better player.
>
> Once you sign with Indiana, you know you are special. He [Knight] thinks you're a special kid. . . . He'll do anything for you, no matter what happens. He's always going to be there for you. It's just apparent the way he looks out for you. It's like all our Mas.

He's kind of like my Ma. When you do something wrong, he just gets so mad. . . . When you don't get the most out of your abilities, he gets so mad. He wants to see you do well so bad that it gets him riled up. . . . I think he has that love for his players that he does everything that he does. You couldn't hate a kid and scream at him to do the right thing. If you didn't like a kid, you'd say "the heck with him." It's very apparent that he has that love.

So there it was out of the mouths of babes. They had witnessed this intense passion of Knight. They had felt it, they had seen their teammates become their brothers, they had seen Knight as a parent, and they had felt his anger. But mostly they had felt his love. I had no more questions.

NOTES

1. Ross Forman, "Hillman's Seen the Good and the Bad," *Terre Haute Tribune-Star*, 5 February 1989.

2. Zach Dunkin, "Joe Hillman—IU Leader Says Baseball Can Wait. . . Until April," *Indianapolis News*, 16 January 1989.

3. Thomas George, "Indiana Strengthened by Setbacks," *New York Times*, 13 March 1989, C5.

4. Eric Ruden, "Senior Spotlight—Joe Hillman," *Hoosier: The Indiana Athletic Review*, 9 March 1989, 122.

5. Ibid.

6. Andy Graham, "Indiana Shuts Off Ellis, Sutton," *Herald-Telephone*, 21 December 1988.

6

Postscript to Jay Edwards

In the fall of 1988 Jay Edwards attended a 10-day substance-abuse program (although Coach Knight wanted the 30-day program). The rehabilitation clinic may have started Edwards toward a change for the better, according to associate athletic director and personal adviser Steve Downing:

> He saw other people at the bottom of the barrel, and they told him, "This is you in so many years." I could see the difference in him. Jay still has a long way to go, but he has taken a giant step. . . . I was really concerned about Jay from day one because he was always in the coach's doghouse.[1]

With his basketball career temporarily up in the air, Edwards enrolled without a scholarship. By October 1988, Edwards was attending class, making his tutoring appointments, and being very cooperative. Coach Knight allowed him to practice with the basketball team the first day of practice.

Knight commented on the current and future status of Jay Edwards during a speech in Kokomo:

> I would like to think, and I really hope more than anytime since I've been at Indiana, that Edwards winds up the best example for kids that we have ever had. . . . We've had some great kids here who never caused us an ounce of trouble. We will never be able to say that about Edwards.
> I told him the other day, "It appears you are trying to do the

right thing." I asked him if it was any harder to do things the right way than to do them the wrong way. He said it was easier to do them the right way, and felt better about himself when he did them the right way.

I told him that my fondest wish would be that when this season is over, no one is a better example for kids.[2]

The Jay Edwards' story is a case in progress. For the spring semester of 1989 Edwards had a restored scholarship. Coach Knight declared, "Edwards has made a conscious effort to succeed. He is now taking pride in what he is doing. He hasn't finished the process but is better in every way." At that time Edwards was living off campus with White freshman Eric Anderson, who was an honor student in high school.

"An Eerie Truth"

In the spring of 1989 things moved rapidly for Jay Edwards. Indiana University won the Big Ten Team Title after being picked by sports writers to finish near the bottom. They were led by Big Ten Player of the Year Jay Edwards. His last-second shots single-handedly turned almost certain losses into wins. About the time I interviewed him, Edwards had decided to turn professional and enter into the NBA draft.

After a disappointing trial camp for prospective top draft choices in Chicago, Edwards was chosen in the second round of the NBA draft by the Los Angeles Clippers. The Clippers are one of the worst teams in professional basketball, with a roster loaded with young players. However, Edwards will be given every opportunity to play immediately.

I asked several people at Indiana University what the interview with Edwards would be like. The comments ranged from an administrator's dismissal ("He'll tell you what you want to hear") to a teammate's praise ("He's a good kid").

Edwards had to pick up his newborn son from its mother. She is neither married to nor living with Jay. So the interview started later than we had planned, and I was at the same time both happy and apprehensive. Happy because we had the time alone and apprehensive because I might still be unable to make sense out of what happened to Edwards at Indiana University.

I wanted to understand Edwards's high school experience. His freshman year he flunked off the basketball team. At the time he had no regrets since "basketball wasn't my number-one priority. . . . I never studied once in four years. I didn't have to. It was easy." Early on Edwards was streetwise and a con man. He learned how to slide by with minimum effort. Knight felt that Edwards had been coddled throughout his young life — that he needed discipline and toughness. It was Knight's plan to help Edwards experience what Knight felt was missing in his life.

In Edwards's first year at IU this pattern would reestablish itself. However, it nearly occurred at the University of Louisville. Edwards wanted to go to Louisville rather than Indiana University because of Coach Denny Crum's "run-and-gun" style of play. With full court pressure and fast breaks as primary ingredients, Crum's Louisville Cardinals play an up-tempo game. This is in direct contrast to Knight's patient offense and half-court man defense. At the last moment, Edwards was persuaded to attend Indiana University by a promise from Knight guaranteeing more running in the Hoosier offense and therefore more scoring opportunities for Edwards. Oddly the main reason Edwards chose IU was Knight's insistence on placing academics foremost in his college career. With a touch of bitterness in his voice, Edwards reflected, "I maybe would have stayed four years at Louisville." I was stunned by this revelation and immediately began to think of Edwards's apparent contradictions concerning academics.

Again in his freshman year at IU Edwards was doing just enough to "get by." When he was finally called in by Knight for cutting class, Edwards found Coach "pissed off, but speaking with a cordial voice. He wasn't smiling but not yelling either. He really gets upset when you miss class. As punishment I ran at 6 A.M. Usually stairs in Assembly Hall — 15 times or so. It wasn't that hard," Edwards said defiantly. Like a child being spanked, he was saying, "It didn't hurt." It was not a question in Edwards's mind whether he did anything right or wrong, but he was immune to their punishment.

Even the tutors Buzz Kurpius supplied for Edwards were not to his liking. They kept after him, questioned him, and rejected his excuses. "I wasn't into them. I wasn't getting anything out of it. I'd rather work with other students than tutors. It's just not me. School wasn't hard for me. It just wasn't my favorite thing. If you just go to class, you can get by," Edwards told me.

Edwards does not like school but is a very bright young man. With little effort, he got B's and C's. Edwards recalled, "Buzz stayed on my back freshman year. . . . I didn't like her, but she was doing her job."

"I used to fib to her a lot."

I wondered how the brick factory job after the freshman year affected him. He admitted the work was hot, dirty, and hard. It was early mornings of stacking concrete blocks and other backbreaking work. He had never experienced anything remotely close to this in his life.

It was manual labor and hard work. I wanted to leave. I left and they called me back. I understood what Coach was trying to do. I worked for two weeks and then I left. I was going to transfer. That job was bullshit. I was risking injury. I was picking up cement blocks and could have broken my back or lost a finger. Coach may not have realized the dangers of the job. I hated it. Taking my car away was cool but not the brick factory job.

At a meeting with the coaching staff, Steve Downing, and Edwards, Edwards was finally talked into coming back to IU for his sophomore year. He was on the verge of transferring to another college but instead made a wise decision and decided to try again.

The factory job became one more story of the deadlock in the Knight-Edwards duel. Neither side seemed to be able to budge or to understand the other's position. The relationship was professional, not personal. There was much missing. Without a breakthrough in communication, they could never maximize what could be gained from the union. What remained was strictly a basketball relationship.

Edwards was doing well in school up until the time he made his unexpected decision to leave IU and seek entrance into the NBA. He presented several items for his academic turnaround and wanted to pass this knowledge to future student-athletes:

Being on time for everything is important. At first I didn't do that. Also going to class and hearing the material is usually sufficient to get by. You also have to get the assignments turned in on time. I would also suggest a syllabus to keep track of everything. It's really me and my head, telling myself "to do it."

Was this what some had warned me about—what I wanted to hear? These items are things Edwards was not doing. It was merely a list.

In spite of Edwards's dislike for Buzz Kurpius, had he clung to some of her tenets? Was he taking something away from IU that she instilled in him?

Although it was clear that Edwards did not like school and perhaps should not have been in college, it was surprising to hear him say that he probably would have finished all four years at Louisville. Everyone, including Jay's mother Rosemary, was caught off guard by his decision to jump to the NBA. Rosemary Edwards recalls:

I don't really know what his thoughts are along those lines. I'm not commenting because I don't know. I think he's been thinking about that [playing in the NBA] ever since he's been in grade school.

I would rather he stay in school. . . . Jay will soon be 21, and I can't stop him from doing anything.

Jay won't do anything that will hurt IU because IU has been very good to Jay. He has enjoyed the season. If he was to leave, he would want to leave on the very best of terms with IU and with Coach Knight.[3]

Edwards admitted to me that he and his mother were very close, but for some reason she was left out on this important career decision of his. He did not notify Coach Knight but informed Steve Downing instead.

Edwards's reasons for leaving school early are closely tied to his relationship with Knight. There is a hidden hurt in his voice when the subject of Knight's love is broached:

Knight felt I was a smart enough player. He only had to tell me one time not to do something. He never yelled at me as far as basketball was concerned. He understood me as a player and never layed into me once; however, it was normal for him to yell at some of the other guys. I got mad at Todd [Jadlow] sometimes. I tried to look at Coach's love. He loves you as a person.

Suddenly Edwards switched emotions and he brought up the nagging team MVP problem. This was something he wanted to address or at least to put on record. The tone of his voice indicated deep hurt. He began to talk about the basketball banquet.

There he sat with some teammates through the ceremony anxiously awaiting the announcement of the IU team's MVP. The topic had even been broached nationally by television sportscaster Dick Vitale, who was boosting Edwards for the award. But Coach Knight had another idea. He announced that the award would go to senior captain Joe Hillman.

Edwards told me, "Next thing Coach says something that hurts you. He told me I was the best player he ever had, but then he gave the MVP to Joe Hillman. I wanted to get up and leave when I heard that. That hurt."

Edwards's older brother and family spokesperson James, a Muncie, Indiana policeman mirrored those comments: "Indiana never has given Jay a fair shake—ever. He does good, you know he's the best player on the team. Period. And they say Joe Hillman is. It's pathetic."[4] It was clear that the MVP snub was a slap in the face to the Edwards family.

I suggested to Edwards that perhaps Knight was honoring a senior (Hillman) with the award for his leadership, and Jay's time would come. He quickly countered my argument by explaining that former star player Steve Alford was the team MVP four years in a row. "Steve Alford ain't the player that I am. I would beat all his records if I would have stayed. I played against him. He worked harder than I do, but I can do more things than him." Alford had been an Indiana hero who led the Hoosiers to a national championship and was now an NBA player. Alford was an honor student. There was much about Alford that Edwards may have envied.

I tried to keep to one topic and again asked Edwards to elaborate on this unique relationship with Knight. He was evasive but still revealed the distant respect each had for the other. Like two warring boxers, they respected the other's skills, but neither would go deeper in the relationship.

Coach Knight was my coach. Period. He always would call me in for advice on other players, on my teammates. I haven't gone in to talk to him about leaving for the pros. I will eventually go and see him. . . .

As far as leaving school now, I was worried that Knight would sit me down. He's bringing in all these good players. I saw him sit Keith Smart down. That could happen to me. I couldn't take that. Also my class of sophomore guards has five or six All-American prospects. If I go now I don't have to compete against them. Right now there are only three or four guards coming out of college that are rated higher than me. I could jump over a couple of them in the Chicago tryout camp next week. This is the best time for me to leave. . . .

I'm going to try to get my degree. It would be crazy to throw away the two years I've put in here. I will try to graduate in either criminal justice or recreational management. I would like to be a coach someday. I understand the game a lot.

Edwards was arrogant and confident about his athletic abilities. He respected Knight but was not close to him or anyone else on the coaching staff. His perceptions about his problems and future show the signs of serious thinking and inner reflection. Edwards was an enigma.

The more I listened to Edwards, the more the connections with Knight and Buzz appeared. Edwards carries the vestiges of those relationships with him. The philosophy, no matter how bitterly he originally fought it, may now be a part of him forever.

Or has anything sunk in? Did any of this get to Jay? I was unable to sense what lay behind those eyes. Did he really feel, understand, believe, and grow? Who knows? I had failed with him, as perhaps Knight and Buzz had. I really didn't know him. Jamal I knew. Eric, Matt, Joe, and the others I could understand—but not Jay Edwards. He seemed to want to change his image:

As a freshman I didn't think about being a role model. Now I'll go to the old folks home in the morning. Bring a portable goal, shoot some baskets, and sign autographs. I've talked to high school kids. I don't hang around with the wrong people anymore.

I don't drink anymore. It's been over two weeks now. I quit. I saw my career going down because of marijuana and alcohol.

Wait a minute. He quit drinking two weeks ago, attended a rehab four or five months prior to that, and is just now quitting? Was Edwards conning himself now?

There were so many shifts and swings of emotions, contradictory information, and deep-seated feelings. I did not know what to make out of him.

He is such a graceful, free, and easy athlete. He glides where others seem to be physically in stress. Edwards is athletically like mercury — beautiful, shiny, and certain.

He summed up his experiences with Knight and IU:

Sometimes I surprise myself. . . . I guess the thing is I'm never afraid to try and surprise myself. Playing here at Indiana is not always easy. There can be so much restriction that you wonder if you are really growing the way in the game that you should. And then when you sit back and you look it over, you see it's a system that works. It's like an eerie truth.[5]

NOTES

1. Kevin Ellison and Matt Solinsky, "Edwards Closes Book on Rocky IU Career," *Indiana Daily Student*, 30 March 1989, 1.

2. Will McDonough, "Knight Says No to Hall," *Boston Globe*, 3 November 1988, 45.

3. Ellison and Solinsky, "Edwards Closes Book," 1.

4. "Knight Believes Edwards Won't Reconsider," *Louisville Courier-Journal*, 1 April 1989, p. B3.

5. Thomas George, "Indiana Strengthened by Setbacks," *New York Times*, 13 March 1989, C5.

7

The IU Record and Comparisons

When at thirty, I want to "dash the cup to the ground," wherever I may be
I'll come to have one more talk with you.
                                          The Brothers Karamazov

The most comprehensive NCAA study thus far of student-athletes is
the $1.75 million NCAA project focusing on 42 Division I "schools,"
including 2,925 male athletes and 1,158 nonathletes. It shows a trend
concerning athletes that has long been thought to be true and clears
up earlier contradictions among researchers. On December 7, 1988,
the *Chronicle of Higher Education* ran the following:

> Student-athletes come to college less well-prepared academically
> and have lower grade-point averages in college than extracur-
> ricular students . . . . Football and basketball players are different
> from other student-athletes in many ways. Football and basket-
> ball players spend more time in their sports, receive more full-
> cost athletic grants, perceive what money they have for personal
> use as less adequate . . . perform more poorly academically and
> feel less capable of meeting their academic demands. Football
> and basketball players in more successfully-competitive
> programs are at the extremes on many of these measures.[1]

The survey found that football and basketball players spend 30 hours
a week during the season on sports and 25 hours a week on their
academic studies. The off-season data for athletes are nearly the same.
Student-athletes also miss two classes per week during the sports
season. The general student population does not have these distrac-

tions. In the more successfully competitive programs, football and basketball players perform academically less successfully.

For example, 34 percent of the football and basketball players in "big time" programs have been on academic probation, as compared with 26 percent in less successfully competitive programs. The ACT and SAT scores and GPAs of football and basketball players are far lower than other sports athletes and lower than participants in other extracurricular (nonathletic) activities. These extracurricular activities include journalism, music, government, and campus work-study. For example, the SAT scores are 888.3, 919.3, and 990.2 for the three groups, respectively (i.e., football and basketball players, other sports, and extracurricular participants.) Also, the grade-point averages are 2.46, 2.61, and 2.79 for the three groups, in the same order (see Table 1). All indications show that major college basketball players put in enormous amounts of time on their sport and academically do not perform as well as other comparison groups.[2]

There are two separate issues here. First, the high school preparation of basketball players is clearly weaker than the incoming student body at large. This academic weakness can be attributed to a subculture that exists among high school star athletes. Jay Edwards (Chapter

Table 1
The NCAA 1989 Student-Athlete Survey

	ACT Scores	SAT Scores	Current College GPA
Football and basketball players in Division I institutions	18.2	883.3	2.46
Other sport participants	19.2	919.3	2.61
Extracurricular participants (non-athletes)	21.4	990.2	2.79

Source: Reprinted from Douglas Lederman, "Players Spend More Time on Sports Than on Studies, An NCAA Survey of Major College Athletes Finds," *Chronicle of Higher Education,* 7 December 1988: A35.

4) is an example. These athletes are often coddled, have their grades inflated by some teachers, are often excused from class and handing in homework, and generally exist in a BMOC (Big Man on Campus) framework. The message often given to them by some teachers and administrators is "studies don't matter." In addition, the vast majority of these high school star players are Black. Although this book does not address in detail the disadvantages of the inner-city Black student-athlete in high school, enough data are available to indicate even more academic hardships for these young men. The second issue affecting college academic performance is the "killing" schedule and time demands. Sports are a full-time job on our college campuses.

The time demands of the football and basketball players indicate a 60-hour week for these Division I athletes (see Table 2). In addition, the preparedness of entering freshman athletes is lower than other comparison groups. This trend also remains true when GPAs are compared.

To reiterate, enormous time demands are placed on football and basketball players at major colleges, and players tend to be less well

Table 2
Time Demands and Use of Personal Time by Different Groups of Students in Sport Seasons (in hours)

Hours per week spent in:	Football and Basketball Players in Division I Schools	Other Sport Players	Extracurricular Activities (nonsports)
Main sport/activity	30.0	24.6	20.4
Class and labs	13.7	14.0	15.0
Preparing for class	11.6	13.2	12.6
Social activities	9.7	11.4	10.6
Relaxing alone	9.2	11.1	8.3
Extracurricular activities (except main one)	3.7	4.3	6.2
Number of classes missed per week	2.0	2.2	1.1

Source: Reprinted from *NCAA News*, 5 December 1988, 14.

Table 3
Indiana University Basketball Comparative Study, 1972–1989

Categories	Numbers	SAT (Avg.)	ACT (Avg.)	Final College G.P.A.	Top 25%	2nd 25%	3rd 25%	Bottom 25%	Racial Breakdown	Graduation Percentage	Comments
					High School			Rank			
IU Basketball Graduates (using 4 years eligibility)	43	871	21.4	2.73	19 / 47.5%	13 / 32.5%	6 / 15%	2 / 5%	70%/30 White 30%/13 Black	43/48 90%	No high school rank on 3 players.
IU Basketball (Transfers)	23	800	18.25	2.29	6 / 26%	5 / 22%	10 / 43%	2 / 8.6%	56%/13 White 44%/10 Black	12/23 52%	Accurate records are not kept on transfers - 3 are currently in school.
IU Basketball (Non-graduates using 4 years eligibility)	5	Insufficient Data		2.06		1 / 33%	1 / 33%		0 White 5 Black		4 of the 5 are within one semester of graduation - 5th has 130 hours but is missing a required course and is the president of a corporation.
IU Basketball (Not completing 4 years eligibility - non-transfers)	6	719	13	2.27	1 / 25%	2 / 50%	1 / 25%		16%/1 White 84%/5 Black	5/6 84%	2 have no high school data recorded - 2 were injured and unable to complete basketball eligibility, 1 went hardship to NBA.

90

IU Basketball (1989 Senior Class)	6	803.3	20	2.69	1	3	1		6 White	3/6	3 current players have graduated and 2 are in graduate school, 1 is doing a double major; all will graduate in June 1989.
IU Bloomington Cohorts All Students	23.587 Average 51.5% Males 1973-88	960 1981-87	21.7 1982-87	2.83 1983-87	63%	31.5% 1984-88	2.6%	.4%	86% White 5% Black	34% 1978-83 All 5 years: 34% Blacks staying 5 years after matriculation 1972-82. 30% All 4 years after matriculation 52% 1978-83 All 5 years	
National High School Data	87.3% White 8% Black 1985 Freshmen	899 1981-87	18.5 1982-87							31% 42% 1972 Freshmen — Black males White males	
NCAA Division I 1989 Survey (Football/Basketball)		883.3	18.2	2.46 Current G.P.A.						33% 1987 NCAA Survey	

W = White
B = Black
M = Male
FR = Freshmen

Source: Compiled by the author.

prepared academically. According to the 1989 NCAA study, the picture of the successful college basketball program at Indiana University, for example, should be even more gloomy since IU basketball is traditionally a Top Ten national program. The survey suggests an inverse ratio between basketball winning teams and academic prowess.

THE INDIANA UNIVERSITY DATA

Table 3 shows the Indiana University basketball team's outstanding academic success in graduation and beyond graduation during Coach Bobby Knight's tenure. By the end of the 1988–89 season, a total of 48 players had completed their college basketball eligibility. Of this total, 43 had earned their degrees. This group now includes nine advanced degrees: two M.D.'s, one D.D., four master's, and two J.D.'s. Therefore, a remarkable 90 percent of those completing eligibility have earned their diplomas. Among graduates, there are two Phi Beta Kappas.

This table is broken down into those that stayed for four years of eligibility as well as other categories. It would be unfair to look at the 43 graduates of those 48 completing eligibility without looking at the 23 transfers and the 6 players not completing their eligibility.

THE 43 GRADUATES UNDER KNIGHT USING FOUR YEARS OF BASKETBALL ELIGIBILITY

CLASS OF 1972

Rick Ford (B.S. in Physical Education, Master's) — Rick went into coaching and is the head basketball coach at Cascade High School west of Indianapolis.

Joby Wright (B.S. in Physical Education, Master's) — Joby played pro basketball for the NBA's Seattle and San Diego franchises and the ABA's Memphis Tams before going to Italy to play pro ball. He returned to IU in 1978 and completed undergraduate requirements. He is currently an assistant coach for Bob

Knight. He expects to complete degree requirements for his second master's degree in education this academic year.

CLASS OF 1973

Steve Downing (B.S. in Physical Education, Master's) — The Boston Celtics No. 1 pick in 1973, Steve played two years for the Celtics including the 1974 NBA championship season. He then returned to work at Indiana University–Purdue University at Indianapolis where he earned his master's in counseling. He joined IU's Department of Intercollegiate Athletics in 1979 and now is an associate athletic director.

Jerry Memering (B.S. in Business) — Following graduation, Jerry returned to his hometown of Vincennes, Ind., to head up his family's business, Memering Construction, Co.

John Ritter (B.S. in Business) — John worked several years for different divisions of Eli Lilly. He handled color commentary for the Big Ten TV Network before serving as an assistant under Bob Weltlich at Mississippi. The past four years, John has lived south of Indianapolis selling insurance and working as a volunteer assistant coach for area high school basketball teams.

Frank Wilson (B.A. in Zoology, M.D.) — It's now Dr. Frank Wilson, orthopedic surgeon, and he specializes in sports related injuries from his northside Indianapolis practice.

CLASS OF 1975

Steve Ahlfeld (B.A. in Biological Sciences, M.D.) — An orthopedic surgeon, Steve recently opened a clinic in Indianapolis — Ahlfeld Sports Medicine Orthopedic Center. He was chief medical officer for Basketball during the Tenth Pan American Games in Indianapolis in 1987.

Doug Allen (B.S. in Business, Master's) — Doug has been with Yellow Freight of Overland Park, Kan., since graduation. He now serves as branch manager of Yellow Freight's Miami, Fla., operation.

Steve Green (B.A. in Biological Sciences, D.D.S.) — Dr. Steve Green is a dentist practicing in Indianapolis. He pinch hits for John Laskowski as color commentator on the IU Television Network in basketball. Green played four seasons in the ABA and a year in Italy before returning to dental school.

John Kamstra (B.S. in Accounting, C.P.A.) — Kamstra completed his certified public accountant requirements and is associated with Cook Group in Bloomington.

John Laskowski (B.S. in Business) — Laz played two years with the Chicago Bulls. He returned to Indianapolis where he now is in commercial real estate for the Hanover Group. He is in his eighth year with the IU Television Network in basketball and is getting ready for his fourth year as color commentator for the Big Ten Game of the Week.

CLASS OF 1976

Tom Abernethy (B.S. in Business) — Abernethy played with Los Angeles, Golden State and Indiana before spending a year in Italy playing professional basketball. He is now a broker in the marketing department of Thomas & Associates in Indianapolis which deals in industrial real estate, development and property management.

Quinn Buckner (B.S. in Administration) — The Milwaukee Bucks' No. 1 selection, Quinn played 10 years in the NBA with Milwaukee, Boston and Indiana. Quinn now lives in Glendale, Wis., where he is involved in several business ventures. Inducted into the IU Athletic Hall of Fame in 1986, Quinn made his debut with the Big Ten Network and ESPN last season as color commentator.

Jim Crews (B.S. in Business) — Jim served eight years as an assistant coach under IU coach Bob Knight. He's in his fourth year as head basketball coach at the University of Evansville.

Scott May (B.S. in Education) — Now a Bloomington business man, Scott retired from basketball after playing several years in Italy. The Chicago Bulls No. 1 draft pick, Scott played with Chicago, Milwaukee and Detroit before heading for Italy. Scott was inducted into the IU Athletic Hall of Fame in 1986.

Don Noort (B.S. in Management) — Don elected to concentrate on this degree his senior year and now is with a paper company in Lexington, Ky.

Bob Wilkerson (B.S. in Physical Education pending verification from UC) — Seattle drafted Bob No. 1, and he played with the Sonics, Denver, Chicago and Cleveland. Since finishing his degree through Indiana at the University of Colorado last summer, Bob has worked as an assistant coach at Colorado under former IU assistant Tom Miller.

CLASS OF 1977

Kent Benson (B.S. in Recreation) — The Milwaukee Bucks took Kent as the No. 1 pick in the 1977 draft. He played in Milwaukee followed by nearly six years in Detroit before moving on to Utah, then Cleveland. He is currently playing in Europe and resides in Bloomington during the off-season.

CLASS OF 1978

Wayne Radford (B.S. in Business) — Wayne played one year for the Indiana Pacers. He's now associated with the Cook Group in Bloomington.

Jim Wisman (B.S. in Business) — Jim spent four years with Cummins Engine Co. in Columbus, Ind., and now is a vice president with Leo Burnett Advertising in Chicago.

CLASS OF 1979

Scott Eells (B.S. in Recreation) — Scott is part of Cook Group in Bloomington.

CLASS OF 1980

Butch Carter (B.S. in Recreation) — Butch played with Los Angeles, Indiana, New York Knicks and Philadelphia during his NBA career. He coached basketball for two years at the high school where he starred in Middletown, Ohio and is now an assistant coach at Long Beach State University.

Mike Woodson (B.S. in Recreation) — The New York Knicks' No. 1 pick, Woodson played in New York and New Jersey before being traded to Kansas City/Sacramento. The Kings traded him two years ago to the Los Angeles Clippers, and he is now with the Houston Rockets.

CLASS OF 1981

Glen Grunwald (B.S. in Business, JD) — Glen completed his law degree at Northwestern University and is practicing with the firm of Winston & Strawn in Chicago.

Phil Isenberger (B.S. in Business, JD) — Phil completed his law degree at the IU School of Law in Indianapolis and is practicing in Indianapolis.

Eric Kirchner (B.A. in Journalism) — Eric has been with CF Freight since graduation. He's now in Cincinnati, Ohio, where he's been the terminal manager for four years.

Steve Risley (B.S. in Business) — Steve is completing his third year as a sales representative with Pfizer Pharmaceuticals after serving as public affairs assistant for Sen. Dan Quayle (R-Ind.).

Ray Tolbert (B.S. in Recreation) — The No. 1 pick by New Jersey, Ray played for Seattle and Detroit in the NBA and a year in Italy. He played one year in the Continental Basketball Association before being picked up last year by the Los Angeles Lakers. He is now playing with Atlanta.

CLASS OF 1982

Landon Turner (B.S. in Physical Education) — A tragic car accident ended Landon's playing career. He now lives in his hometown of Indianapolis where he is in business for himself.

CLASS OF 1983

Steve Bouchie (B.S. in Education) — Steve is part of his family's agricultural business in Washington, Ind.

Tony Brown — Tony has been back in his hometown of Chicago and serves as president of Euro Capital, Inc., involved with international trade and finance.

Ted Kitchel (B.S. in Management & Administration) — After working in insurance in Kokomo and Indianapolis, Ted is now employed by A.R. Air Freight.

Isiah Thomas (B.A. in Criminal Justice) — Isiah has been a six-year starter for the Detroit Pistons. As his professional career permitted, Isiah completed classwork for his degree which he officially finished last year.

Jim Thomas (B.S. in Forensic Science) — Jim now calls Indianapolis home while pursuing a CBA career.

Randy Wittman (B.S. in Management & Administration) — Atlanta's No. 1 draft pick, Randy played with the Hawks for five years before being traded this past summer to Sacramento. He has one year completed toward a master's degree in urban affairs.

CLASS OF 1984

Cam Cameron (B.S. in Management & Administration) — Cam is an assistant football coach under Bo Schembechler at Michigan working with receivers. He is also nearing completion of his master's in athletic administration.

Chuck Franz (B.S. in Computer Science) — Chuck is associated with Cook Group in Bloomington.

CLASS OF 1985

Dan Dakich (B.A. in Telecommunications) — Dan is in his second year as an assistant coach under Bob Knight and has completed one year toward his master's in college student personnel administration.

Uwe Blab (B.A. in Computer Science and Mathematics) — Uwe was a fourth-year player for the NBA's Dallas Mavericks. He was selected Phi Beta Kappa his senior year at IU. He is now with his second NBA team.

CLASS OF 1986

Winston Morgan (B.S. in Public Recreation) — Winston worked for Yellow Freight in Indianapolis before joining a professional basketball team in Argentina. He is playing this season in Sweden.

Stew Robinson (Completing Degree Requirements) — Stew worked at Yellow Freight in Indianapolis before returning to Bloomington where he is currently employed.

Courtney Witte (B.S. in Public Affairs) — After working in his family's business in Vincennes, Ind. for several years, Courtney is currently with the Indiana Pacers as a broadcast account executive.

CLASS OF 1987

Steve Alford (B.S. in Marketing) — Steve is in his second year with the Dallas Mavericks after being taken in the second round of the professional draft.

Todd Meier (B.S. in Marketing) — Todd has settled in Indianapolis where he is employed by GTE.

Daryl Thomas (Completing Degree Requirements) — Daryl played professional basketball last year in England where he was chosen as England's Player-of-the-Year. After spending the summer working on his degree in Bloomington, Daryl returned to Europe for another year of basketball.

CLASS OF 1988

Steve Eyl (B.A. in Marketing) — Steve has just finished training for his sales representative position with Baxter International Pharmaceutical and Hospital Supplies.

Dean Garrett (Completing Degree Requirements) — Dean was drafted in the second round by the Phoenix Suns last summer.

Keith Smart (Completing Degree Requirements) — Keith was drafted by the Golden State Warriors in the second round of last summer's draft and is now with San Antonio.*

Class sizes differ because there are a fixed number (15) of allowable scholarships in the Big Ten. So if seven players are recruited for the incoming season, there will only be eight scholarships to give out in the next four seasons until the seven graduate.

Among these graduates are the honored conference Academic All–Big Ten selections: John Ritter (three times), Frank Wilson, John Laskowski, Steve Green (twice), Kent Benson (twice), Wayne Radford, Randy Wittman (three times), Uwe Blab (three times), Joe Hillman (three times), and Magnus Pelkowski. Also, the national Academic All-Americans from Knight's players include John Ritter, Steve Green (twice), Kent Benson (twice), Wayne Radford, Randy Wittman (twice), and Uwe Blab.

* "Knight Players After I.U.," *Hoosier: The Indiana Athletic Review.* 9 March 1988, 89, 90. Reprinted with permission.

Of the 43 graduates, 32 are White and 11 are Black. Their majors were:

Physical Education	5
Real Estate Administration	2
English	1
Accounting	2
Zoology	1
Biological Science	2
Transportation and Public Utilities Management	1
General Management	5
Management and Administration	5
Education	1
Recreation	5
Marketing	6
Business	2
Journalism	1
Computer Science	2
Forensic Studies	1
Telecommunications	1

The Black graduates majored in Forensic Studies, Recreation, Criminal Justice, Physical Education, Political Science, Education, General Management, Marketing, and Business. The average GPA for all the graduates was 2.73.

Comparing these numbers with the 1988 NCAA Survey of Student-Athletes shows the remarkable achievements of the Indiana University basketball players. A further comparison with IU cohorts at Bloomington also reveals outstanding success for Knight's graduates (see Table 4).

The numbers in Table 4 indicate that average students attend IU and play basketball but that these student-athletes graduate at enormously higher percentages than the rest of Division I basketball players and much higher than their IU cohorts. Knight does not acquire the best

Table 4
IU Academic Comparison

	ACT	SAT	GPA	Graduation Rate after Four Years Eligibility or Four Years after Matriculation (percent)
IU, Knight's tenure basketball players, (1972–present)	21.4	871 (final)	2.73	90
IU, Bloomington, all full-time students, 1973–88	21.7	960 (final)	2.83	38
NCAA 1988 Survey of Football and Basketball Division I Players	18.2	883.3 (Current)	2.46 (Median)	33 1987 NCAA survey for basketball only, Division I players (entering freshman, 1981)

student-athletes or the worst but a mixture. Knight's players do not all major in Physical Education. In fact, only 5 of the 48 who completed four years of basketball eligibility majored in Physical Education. The majority (23) majored in Business- or Administration-related fields. So nearly 48% of the entire group majored in these two latter areas.

THOSE OF THE 48 COMPLETING FOUR YEARS OF ELIGIBILITY WHO HAVE NOT GRADUATED

This group of nongraduates is composed of five Black former players. The average GPA of all five is 2.06. Four of these five are within one semester of graduation. All four are currently taking courses to graduate in the near future. They have all tried, or are currently trying, to play professional basketball. The fifth member of this group, Tony Brown, serves as president of Euro Capital, Inc., in his hometown of Chicago. Tony has over 130 credits toward a degree but lacks several required courses. This group will probably shrink to just one within the near future.

It is interesting to note that national graduation rates for entering college freshmen from 1972 show a national graduation rate of 31 percent for Black males and 42 percent for White males. Knight's Black players have graduated at near 70 percent (11 out of 16 — with another 4 near completion of their course work for graduation).

THE 23 TRANSFERS OF THE IU BASKETBALL TEAM

> I too was striving to stand among Thy elect, among the strong and powerful, thirsting "to make up the number." But I was awakened and would not serve madness.
>
> *The Brothers Karamazov*

This group is not counted against the 90 percent graduation rate of Knight's players since some leave within weeks of arriving on campus. Players leave Indiana and transfer for a variety of reasons (i.e., injuries, homesick, grades, lack of playing time, family problems, etc.). Larry Bird (Boston Celtic star) arrived in 1974 at Bloomington from the tiny Indiana town of French Lick. Bird stayed at IU for less than two months. He went home to a girlfriend and then became a truck driver. Eventually he enrolled at Indiana State University, graduated, and later became a superstar in professional basketball.

The transfers have a final grade-point average of 2.29 (with a range of 1.41 to 3.21) at IU. The declared majors of this group were:

Physical Education	2
Optometry	1
History	2
Management and Administration	2
Public Affairs	1
Accounting	1
Exploratory	1
Recreation	1
Forensic Studies	1
General Studies	2

The transfers were composed of 10 Black and 13 White athletes. Their average SAT score was 800 (15 players), and 4 players had an ACT score of 18.25. Some players had no test scores recorded. Six of the transfers were in the top quarter of their high school graduating class, five in the second quarter, ten in the third, and one in the bottom quarter. The others had no recorded high school rank. They transferred to institutions such as Providence, North Carolina State, Evansville, Nevada–Las Vegas, Ball State, Auburn, Illinois, Bowling Green, Duke, and Massachusetts. At least ten of these transfers are known to have graduated. Three of these transfers are currently in school. The data on graduation are incomplete since Indiana University does not follow up on the academic progress of their transfers.

What is known of them is that at least two have gone to graduate school and one has a law degree. Another transfer went into the service.

THOSE SIX NOT COMPLETING FOUR YEARS OF BASKETBALL ELIGIBILITY AND REMAINING AT INDIANA UNIVERSITY

This group had five graduates—five Black and one White. Their final grade-point average is 2.27. The three who took the SAT had an average score of 719. Two of these six were injured and were unable to complete their basketball careers; however, both of these student-athletes graduated. One player, Isiah Thomas, left IU after his sophomore year to play professionally with the Detroit Pistons of the NBA. Isiah graduated with a B.A. in Criminal Justice last year, five years after his classmates graduated.

In explaining the academic success of his IU basketball players, Bobby Knight asserts that they learn much more than basketball fundamentals. In an interview in November 1982 Knight reflected on his work ethic with his players:

I think that, in being demanding, you teach players to expect better results from themselves, and you develop in them a greater willingness to put much more into what they're doing than most people would. If you place great demands on players, you force them to put more into things, and subsequently, they get more out of them. And I think this carries over into other things that they do. If you don't expect just to be competitive, but you expect to win, then I think a player's ability to succeed is enhanced by the fact that as a player he was expected to win. Losing is something that you don't expect, don't tolerate. As a result, I think a player is less likely to wind up in situations where he loses away from basketball. Second, for a person to be successful and to be motivated toward success, there has to be a lot of self-respect involved. A kid who goes through our program, where he is a well-respected member of both the athletic community and the academic community, develops a lot of self-esteem. Then, in turn, a confidence develops that enables him to compete in business or industry or whatever. Our kids have been pretty successful in competing away from basketball, and I think that the demands we've placed on them and the fact that we have said you've got to work harder because we expect more out of you than some place else has a great bearing on this. I've talked to former players, and this is a thread that runs through all of their conversations.[3]

The voices of former players are equally important in analyzing the academic success of IU student-athletes. Steve Downing, current IU associate athletic director and All-American in 1973, recalled:

Before Coach Knight came to IU, I was just an average student. When I met him, he didn't talk basketball. He just said, "Hey, I think you can do better academically, and if you do that, it'll make you a lot better ball player."[4]

Phil Isenberger, lawyer and member of the 1981 NCAA Championship Team, explained:

Coach Knight and Buzz Kurpius made me realize how important it was to get a degree to promote a future beyond basketball. That's what led to law school. Now I find the basketball program still helps me. In my line of work, there is absolutely nothing more important than preparation. The benefits of Coach Knight's basketball program can really be applied to so many different things.[5]

Steve Ahlfeld, M.D., and member of the 1973 NCAA Final Four Team, felt this way:

The thing I feel is so impressive about Coach Knight's record at Indiana is that the national championships, the Big Ten championships, the winning records are all there along with a record of players achieving nearly a 100 percent graduation rate. That combination is one that I don't think has been duplicated in the past 16 years at any other place.[6]

Steve Green, D.D.S. and All-American in 1974, said of Knight:

Coach Knight's desire for us to excel in the classroom, as well as on the court, is basic to everything he does. He'll ensure that you'll get the best education possible when you come to Indiana. And, he'll be the best ally you'll have from the time you enter Indiana, throughout your career, then for the rest of your life.[7]

And finally, James Thomas, businessman and All–Final Four Member of the 1981 NCAA Championship Team, summed up what he had learned:

Coach Knight is demanding, but life is demanding after you graduate. I learned to take each day as an opportunity to improve upon the skills I needed to improve upon. I still try to do that now as an individual in society.[8]

These numbers and people dramatize the overwhelming success of Knight's tenure at Indiana University. Players graduate with meaningful degrees from Indiana regardless of their color or their high school background. Those graduates also tend to be extremely successful in the business world.

Those who continue with basketball for four years and/or who stay at Indiana University graduate at an astonishing rate of 90 percent. It also appears that five of the six players who finished their eligibility will graduate in the near future.

In the summer of 1988, Bobby Knight gave a speech to the Louis-ville, Kentucky, High School Coaches Association. He said he would give up all three of the IU NCAA championships to see 35-year-old Bob Wilkerson walk down the aisle and graduate before the as-sembled basketball coaches. That summer, former IU and NBA basketball player Bob Wilkerson graduated 12 years after his class of 1976. Knight paid for Wilkerson and his mother to fly to Bloomington for the graduation ceremony. Knight had promised Mrs. Wilkerson her son would get a diploma. He often promises this to parents of his players.

Rarely, does he not make good.

In the summer of 1987, Isiah Thomas's mother came to the gradua-tion ceremony to pick up her son's diploma. Isiah was in the NBA championship playoffs with the Detroit Pistons. He had left IU after his sophomore season in 1981 to play professional basketball. Knight had promised Mrs. Thomas that Isiah would graduate.

Those six who have not graduated as of yet will be hounded by Knight until they finish. Knight saw one of them at Assembly Hall during the summer of 1988 during a pickup basketball game. Knight yelled across the gym floor for all to hear, "Stew, have you got your ass back in class yet?" The point was made. Knight has promises to keep. Promises to mothers.

Tables 5 and 6 show what the Indiana University program has been emphasizing — meaningful degrees and high graduation rates regard-less of race. Whatever the backgrounds student-athletes bring to IU, the vast majority earn their diplomas at IU. Knight and his staff relentlessly keep after the players to complete their school work, attend class, and graduate.

In spite of the recent studies showing the unusual time demands on student-athletes in big-time college sports, the Indiana basketball players are successful in meeting academic demands. Behind the programs and the successful numbers are the people driving and directing them. In philosophy and motivation Coach Knight and Buzz Kurpius lead by example.

Table 5
IU Totals for Bob Knight's Tenure, 1972–Present

Categories	Numbers	SAT (Avg.)	ACT (Avg.)	Final College G.P.A.	High School Rank — Top 25%	2nd 25%	3rd 25%	Bottom 25%	Racial Breakdown	Graduation Percentage	Comments
All IU Basketball Players Under Knight	83	835 (54 Players) Three players took both tests, some scores were not recorded.	19.4 (17 Players)	2.52 (78 Players)	27 36% 24/27 graduated, other 3 transferred, unknown if two have graduated.	24 32% 18/24 75% graduated, 1 currently in school.	19 25% 12/19 63% graduated, 1 more expected to graduate in 1989.	5 6% 3/5 60% graduate, 1 more expected in 1989.	60%/50 White 40%/33 Black	66/83 79.5%	This includes anyone playing for Knight (including transfers.)
							Only 75 have recorded high school rank.				
White Players	50	929 (37 Players) 2 took both, 4 didn't take either.	22.3 (11 Players)	2.71 (48 Players)					N/A	44/50 88%	White Graduation rate.
Black Players	33	631 (17 Players) 9 had no information.	14 (6 Players) 1 took both,	2.24 (30 Players)					N/A	22/33 66%	Black graduation rate. Three are undergraduates still in school, 5 are within 2 courses and are close to finishing.

pl   =   players
n.a. =   not applicable
Source: Compiled by the author.

Table 6
Racial Differences in IU Graduation Rates for Basketball Players during Coach Knight's Tenure

IU players racial origin	Category of IU basketball player	Number of players in category	Percentage graduating
White	Those using four years eligibility	30	100%
Black		18	72.2% (all those not graduating are within one semester of graduation)
White	IU basketball transfers	13	54%
Black		10	50% (3 are undergraduates; fate of some transfers unknown)
White	Players (not completing	1	100%
Black	four years of eligibility — nontransfers)	5	80%
White	Current 1989 senior class	6	100% (3 scheduled to graduate; 3 have graduated)
Black		0	—
White	Totals during Knight's tenure	50	88%
Black		33	66.6%

NOTES

1. Douglas Lederman, "Players Spend More Time on Sports Than on Studies, An NCAA Survey of Major-College Athletes Finds," *Chronicle of Higher Education*, 7 December 1988, A38.

2. "A Study of the Student-Athlete," *The NCAA News*, 5 December 1988, 13–16.

3. David England, "Athletics, Academics, and Ethics: An Interview with Bob Knight," *Phi Delta Kappan*, November 1982, 163.

4. "Knight Players after Indiana," *Indiana University Basketball: A Winning Tradition*, (I. U. Department of Intercollegiate Athletics, Bloomington, Ind. 1988) 24.

5. Ibid., 25.

6. Ibid., 26.

7. Ibid.

8. Ibid., 27.

8

Conclusion

You will see great sorrow, and in that sorrow you will be happy. This is my
last message to you: in sorrow seek happiness. Work, work unceasingly.
                                                       The Brothers Karamazov

The basketball world has come far from the peach basket attached to
the barn door. Today's college sports represent a litany of failure, a
failure of young men. Failures come from high school transcripts being
altered so that young players will be eligible for college. Failure is an
athlete attending college for four years of sports eligibility and finding
himself without a lucrative professional career and diploma. What
remains instead is the reality of finding work without a diploma,
without job skills, and with a six-feet-ten-inch frame on a Black body.
Daily the mass media grind out the latest college infractions and
NCAA penalties, but the beat goes on. One good recruited player
brings all the riches and plunder a coach or school needs to realize a
full gymnasium of fans and wealthy and happy alumni. Knight, the
spirit of another age, the spirit of Ulysses S. Grant and Woody Hayes
(former Ohio State legendary football coach and disciplinarian), the
spirit of hard work, discipline, and sweat on the brow, finds himself in
this calculated world.

Jay Edwards, Kevin Ross, and thousands more like them are the
subjects of adulation, potential exploitation, and helping and oftentimes misguided hands. They are subject to the conflicting values of a
basketball world gone mad. The tragedy of Black athletes in basketball
who can hit a jump shot in your face, soar to block a shot, or run the
floor with athletic ability is that these souls are often the overwhelmed

victims of recruiters, gamblers, coaches, teachers, and Bylaw 5–2–(j).
These kids, as sociologist Harry Edwards and others have documented, don't graduate as often as their White teammates and have a
lesser chance in acquiring a meaningful job without a diploma than
their peers. How does one make sense of these horrifying national
statistics of student-athletes?

Knight ignores the harsh and oftentimes deprived backgrounds of
some of his players; it is no excuse for academic failure. Some urban
sociologists would provide excuses for these kids — but not Knight. He
sees Blacks as able. They are treated as full human beings without *a
way out.* When Indiana University was considering a mandatory attendance policy (similar to the University of Wisconsin), Knight saw this
as a way of singling out athletes. Blacks would especially be affected
by the policy because they are disproportionately represented in
sports.

Coach Knight has few rules for his team. There is an underlying
philosophy that everyone must operate by: *Do your best.* All else is
unacceptable. No one can be happy with less than his best effort. This
ongoing struggle for personal perfection goes beyond basketball, the
classroom, graduation, and the business world. Living life daily by
some personal pride and standards is integral.

Knight has said of his philosophy:

> If you were to ask me to boil this whole thing down to the simplest
> form, it might be this: in order to be any good, you got to know
> what you're bad at, and so you play your strengths and play away
> your weaknesses. But somebody's got to tell you what the hell
> your weaknesses are and somebody's got to tell you the mistakes
> you're making. If they don't do that, you have no chance.[1]

The success of the Indiana University athletes under the care of
Knight and Buzz Kurpius is easy to document. The numbers jump out
at you, defying belief.

If you include Knight's six years as the West Point basketball head
coach, of all players using four years of basketball eligibility, only five
have not graduated. That is *five* players in 23 years! That number is
soon to shrink to just *one*, since four of them are playing professional
basketball and just need a course or two to finish. More startling,

however, is the fifth player — Tony Brown — class of 1983. Tony has over 130 credits toward graduation (IU requires 120 credits), but Tony lacks a required course. To be precise, it is President Tony Brown of Euro Capital, Inc., an international trade and finance corporation. If West Point is included in Coach Knight's graduation percentage of four-year players, the mark of graduation hovers near 93 percent. Omit the West Point tenure, and Knight's 17 years at IU with four-year players is still an amazing 90 percent.

Now include all those at IU that transferred, became injured, or just quit basketball. These groups number 83 players — all either recruited to play basketball or just walked on and made the team. Of this group, at least 66 already graduated — 80 percent — with 3 still in school as undergraduates at other institutions. Included in this group is Landon Turner, class of 1982, who was involved in a tragic car accident following his junior year. He became a paraplegic but still graduated with the support of Knight and Kurpius.

Statistics concerning graduation rates for Division I sports programs are usually kept in one of two ways. First, entering freshmen recruited, on scholarship, are followed up five years later to see if they have graduated. In the NCAA's most recent survey, 33 percent of the football and basketball players recruited graduate within five years. The other way to keep a graduation percentage is to examine those athletes staying with the program and using their four years of eligibility. In this latter manner the coach and academic support have a chance to influence and develop the student-athlete. Athletes that stay with Coach Knight and Buzz Kurpius graduate at over a 90 percent margin. By comparison, IU cohorts, four years after matriculation, graduate at a rate of 38 percent and five years after matriculation, the cohorts have a 52 percent graduation rate.

The numbers are powerful testimony when one considers that several big-time colleges have not graduated a single basketball player in a decade.

Comparisons with IU cohorts, Division I athletes, and national graduate rates show an exceptional success story. Knight's players graduate at a rate of better than 2:1 above the national average. At the end of the 1989 summer, the graduation rate for Knight's players will soar close to 100 percent. In a world where a 40 percent graduation rate is considered high, Knight is graduating players at almost 100 percent—this for 23 years of coaching. The process of success is ongoing and relentless. When players arrive at Assembly Hall to see the championship banners swaying from the ceiling, they are rushed off to sit in Buzz's courtside office. This office, with a computer filled with the data of every athlete ever to play for Knight at Indiana, is decorated with artwork by six-feet-ten-inch basketball player Magnus Pelkowski. One work, of a peasant pushing a cart in a Central American city, is inscribed in a touching, respectful, and thanking manner by Magnus to Buzz. Kurpius is the elementary school teacher that all these young men had as boys. She is unflinching, tough, thorough, and compassionate. Sometimes she demonstrates her love and care by scolding.

When White basketball player Joe Hillman, a fifth-year starter for Knight, was in the baseball Arizona Instructional League in early September, Buzz signed Joe up for three independent study courses. These were Afro-American studies, Drugs and Baseball, and Business Management. She procured his texts and sent them out to him in Arizona so he could keep up with his classes.

Indiana University is a public institution that admits a wide variety of students with different academic skills. Knight's players run the gamut of educational preparation and abilities. Whether they come as pampered high school stars with little concern for attending class and jump-shooting ability like Jay Edwards, or arrive with Phi Beta Kappa potential and no hands (Uwe Blab), all are treated fairly.

Not equally but fairly.

Knight finds the switch to turn them into successful players and students. Knight (without statistics to back his claim) feels his players are the "most successful" beyond graduation of any Division I basketball program. By *successful* Knight means attainment of positions of importance in the work force, earning potential, and employer satisfaction with his players' preparation and effort.

More than the numbers are the individual stories of Knight and his staff (especially Buzz Kurpius) following these players, pulling and tugging at them, punishing them, praising them, shaking them, scolding them, caring for them, being compassionate with them, and mostly loving them.

The stories are summed up in the ongoing two-year struggle to get Jay Edwards to take pride in his course work. Edwards had been treated as a full human being. He had his car taken away from him. He had been given a dirty job in a brick factory over the summer. He had to go through drug rehabilitation and then Alcoholics Anonymous meetings. The Edwards story is ongoing. It is a process.

The elements of the Indiana University program leading to graduation involve both people and activities. No academic success is possible without support and leadership in a hands-on fashion by the basketball coach. The players, in general, will not work for the diploma unless the head coach constantly emphasizes the need for an education. Players must know the coach will take action and penalize them for cutting class, missing assignments or tutoring sessions, or working below ability. The head coach sets the tone, philosophy, and principles under which athletes will function as *student-athletes.*

The coaching staff, too, cannot function successfully in graduating players without a vigilant academic support team. This team must monitor athletic eligibility, course selection, grades, class attendance, and tutoring sessions. The coaching staff and academic support team work as a unit with constant communication and similar goals. Each group must have a certain amount of power over the players. The coaches can make the athletes run at six in the morning, make them sit out games, or take their scholarships away. Academic support personnel must have the right to see players before or after practice to discuss problems, set up tutoring sessions, or complete makeup work.

Players must realize failure to cooperate with the academic support staff means digressions will be reported to the head coach and appropriate disciplinary action will follow. This sharing of power and punishment between coaches and academic support staff presents a united front to the student-athlete.

The activities of a successful program involve monitoring class attendance, tutoring sessions, mandatory study halls for those in difficulty, periodic check of grades and progress during the semester from the instructor, individual counseling and guidance, sessions on use of the library and note taking, and team meetings that reinforce goals, attitudes, and work habits. Specialists should be hired to tutor in each subject area. One assistant basketball coach should be given liaison responsibilities between the academic support staff and the head coach.

Teachers, administrators, and parents are all part of the process. Teachers are invited to attend practice, meet with members of the coaching staff and academic support people, and watch their student-athletes at practice. Administrators are asked to support a higher academic standard for the student-athlete than for the general student body as well as disciplinary codes for those athletes that fall below the coaches' and academic support team's expectations.

Parents are a central part of the process as well. They are asked to turn their sons over to the coaches and academic support people with regard to their educational progress. Parents are encouraged to support the decisions, discipline, and actions of the academic and basketball staff.

Among the reasons the IU program leads to a much higher gradua-tion rate than comparison groups are vigilance, tenacity, and con-tinuity of the people behind the programs. Knight doggedly keeps after Bob Wilkerson for 13 years to finish his course work. Buzz sets up independent study courses and transferable college work for Isiah Thomas of the Detroit Pistons. Isiah, after leaving IU following his sophomore year, takes courses at Wayne State University and IU independent studies. He graduates three years later. Summers at Bloomington are a reunion of former and current players completing course work to acquire a degree. Knight helps players with summer jobs and incentives to continue, whereas Kurpius extracts the proper courses that count toward graduation.

As many of the players have stated to me, it would be unthinkable to come to Indiana and not earn a degree knowing that almost all the former athletes have succeeded in doing so. These last two episodes are recurring for Knight and Kurpius. From early on in the high school recruiting process, Knight stresses the importance of getting a diploma, states what will be expected and what will not be tolerated academically for the student-athlete, and thereby establishes an un-written contract for the new recruit. This academic vigilance continues during the off-season as well as the summer months.

Knight also speaks to these young men about success beyond graduation. He wants the preparation, organization, and discipline that are required to be an intelligent athlete transferable to an intel-ligent student and eventually to an intelligent businessman. Knight presents a philosophy that is *living*. A philosophy that carries one through all avenues of life. While living his philosophy, Knight hopes his players will better be able to formulate their own.

The uniqueness of the IU process is twofold: (1) the lifelong diligence and support of the IU people and (2) the philosophical level that elevates all concerned parties. Other colleges have roughly the same daily programs as Indiana, but few have the vigilant follow-up. The other critical missing ingredient in many places is the effective leadership in academics of the head basketball coach. The successful coach leads by decisions and actions tied to some guiding principles and a philosophy.

It would be false to conclude that IU admits better entering student-athletes than other public institutions. The data in the charts in fact show that the basketball players have lower entering SAT scores than the IU Bloomington cohorts and lower than the average Division I basketball and football player SAT scores. The charge that IU admits smarter and better athletes is unfounded on two points. First, the data clearly show that IU admits student-athletes with a great range of abilities but still manages to graduate a vast majority. Second, regarding IU's recruiting better athletes to win, it is widely believed by most knowledgeable observers that the opposite is in fact true. Knight, in general, gets below-average players to overachieve on the court, in the classroom, and after graduation.

IMPLICATIONS

> Here when I stay with you from time to time, my life gains a kind of reality and that's what I like most of all. You see, like you, I suffer from the fantastic and so I love the realism of earth.
>
> *The Brothers Karamazov*

This book has been an attempt to look at a public institution that has one of the best records in winning basketball games on a big-time level and at the same time graduates an amazingly high percentage of its players. Leadership can be effective in many forms. The programs and processes can be duplicated.

As John Ryan, former president of Indiana University, related to me:

Coach [Bob Knight] is unique. He prizes it. He's one of a kind
and he resists mightily an attempt to place a stamp on him. Some
of Bob's affected attitude stems from a force within him. An
inclination that is not a "me-too-er." He doesn't yield to the
pressure of any group. Bob is exceptionally intelligent, bright,
perceptive, and logical.

Knight is less tolerant and forgiving of people who let down and
stop short of achieving their end. Knight doesn't say, "I'm close
enough to success. I don't have to drive hard anymore." He
believes "however good you are today is not good enough for
tomorrow." He will think this way forever.

Knight is unique; unique cannot be duplicated. The program
probably succeeds in major part because of Coach Knight. His
philosophy and character are so strong; he pulls everyone up to a level
higher than one would imagine. Chuckie White, a Black junior college
transfer currently playing for IU, says of Knight, "Nothing good comes
easy. He's so hard on players that he cares about them. He gets on you
to help you."

How does one duplicate a man who often is left in front of a
Bloomington hospital to visit patients when the team is returning
from a road basketball game? How does one duplicate a man that
gives his one-time star player Landon Turner a new mission in life
after a tragic accident—to graduate and continue growing? One of
the academic advisers to the basketball players, Lacenda Fox, suf-
fered the untimely death of her husband. Once a week, no matter
where Knight is, he calls her young son to encourage him. These are
a few of the dozens of anecdotes that I discovered in trying to
understand Knight and his program.

"How many of you are reading a book right now?" he demands.
He holds up the biography, *Vince*, which he is reading. "How
many of you read books about people that succeed or fail? If you
don't, how the hell do you know what's in success and what's in
failure?"...

"I don't just want you people to win in basketball," he says. "I
want you to win in everything that you do."[2]

Knight constantly reads, constantly reminds his team of the value of books. The team becomes a fund-raiser for the library when they play in three scrimmages throughout the state of Indiana. The central tangible asset of education is the *book.* Everyone must respect the *book.* Learning is accomplished through reading. Reading brings one closer to goals of success at whatever one does.

Many schools have an academic support process (i.e., the tutors, study tables, attendance checks, and some form of discipline). However, it doesn't work for a lot of places. The driving force behind the process must be the head coach. The head coach has to have a philosophy—something he or she believes in, something by which to live a life. This philosophy has to be in the forefront of every action of the program. It has to be often cold and logical and, at the same time, warm and compassionate. It has to be strong and disciplined but well meant and clearly understood.

Knight stands as a model in this regard.

He stands perhaps like a figure from one of the many biographies he reads. How would you know what success is unless there were a *Knight* to measure yourself by?

Not every leader can or should be a Knight. Everyone should live by his or her philosophy, use his or her strengths and personality. There are many ways of being an effective leader. The specific personal characteristics of Knight are not necessarily required to maintain a successful program, but successful programs do appear to depend on some mix of personal qualities that work for the coach involved. In some other cases, success may depend on the institutional traditions.

John Thompson, coach of Georgetown University, is six feet ten inches, Black, rather quiet, and a successful leader in graduating his basketball players. In the recent controversy surrounding Proposition 42 (a stricter version of Proposition 48 that would take away financial aid for student-athletes who did not meet the academic requirements), Thompson spoke out against this policy. As a symbolic gesture he did not coach or sit on the bench for two games immediately following the furor. Thompson is not Knight. He doesn't have to be. However, they share many of the same qualities for effective leadership. They stand for something and put that in front of winning and losing basketball games. They care about their student-athletes. This *care* takes on different forms for both of these great coaches, but it is certainly effective.

Competent leaders are found in varying sizes, temperaments, styles, manners, and articulation. What appears common among them are their commitment to graduation, intensity, care about the worth of each individual entrusted to them, hard work and dedication, and an espoused philosophy critical to their lives.

Success may not even require a charismatic figure such as Knight. The University of Virginia has done an exceptional job of graduating players without an apparent central figure as a leader. It may well be that the institution and its tradition play a major role in graduating athletes in some schools. Notre Dame and Duke (although private schools) are highly competitive basketball powers that graduate unusually high percentages of their players. Again, both schools do not seem to have the charismatic leader but perhaps have tradition and a strong academic support program in place.

Another reason for the need for unusually strong personalities and values is that the governing body of college athletes, the NCAA, is inadequate in supporting academic achievement or controlling unscrupulous coaches. The NCAA appears to be limited in manpower to police some coaches or university presidents who sacrifice their students' academic careers for the riches and glory of winning basketball programs. Changing NCAA rules to prohibit exploitation of the athletes and empowering the NCAA to level severe penalties for rule violations would go far in changing the spirit of the term *student-athlete*. The NCAA could force the emphasis on the "student" in *student-athlete*.

Indiana University, under the leadership of Coach Bob Knight and the academic support team headed by Buzz Kurpius, has done a truly amazing job in getting student-athletes to graduate. The program is similar to those in many colleges throughout the country. The difference is the people pushing the process.

This book highlighted a program that wins in two very important ways—first through graduation and second, through basketball games. Leadership is multifaceted and requires a certain blend of qualities and strengths that this book does not examine. This is an atypical study of something *good* in college athletics—of success in academics.

NOTES

1. Joan Mellen, *Bob Knight: His Own Man* (New York: Donald I. Fine, 1988), 188.
2. Ibid., 180–81.

A Memory of Childhood

You must know that there is nothing higher and stronger and more wholesome and good for life in the future than some good memory, especially a memory of childhood, of home. People talk to you a great deal about your education, but some good, sacred memory, preserved from childhood, is perhaps the best education. If a man carries many such memories with him into life, he is safe to the end of his days, and if one has only one good memory left in one's heart, even that may sometimes be the means of saving us.

The Brothers Karamazov

Appendix: List of Interviewees

IU COACHES:

Bob Knight, Head Coach
Dan Dakich, Assistant Coach
Ron Felling, Assistant Coach
Taylor "Tates" Locke, Assistant Coach
Joby Wright, Assistant Coach

IU BASKETBALL PLAYERS:

Eric Anderson
Mike D'Aloisio
Jay Edwards
Joe Hillman
Todd Jadlow
Lyndon Jones
Jamal Meeks
Matt Nover
Magnus Pelkowski
Chuckie White

ATHLETIC DEPARTMENT:

Ralph Floyd, Athletic Director
Steve Downing, Associate Director
Mike Wolinsky, Administrative Assistant
Kit Klingelhoffer, Sports Information Director
Eric Ruden, Assistant Sports Information Director
Tim Garl, Basketball Trainer
Julio Salazar, Head Manager

ACADEMIC SUPPORT STAFF:

Elizabeth "Buzz" Kurpius, Head of Academic Support
Mary Rose, Head Assistant
Anita House, Assistant
Marge Belisle, Head of Tutoring
Bobbie Robertson, Tutor
Terrie Keith, Tutor

FACULTY:

Sam Newburg, Retired (formerly Physical Education)
Lacenda Fox, Aquatics Coordinator; Adviser to Players
Harry Pratter, Professor Emeritus, Law School
William Wiggins, Professor of Afro-American Studies
Gloria Gibson-Hudson, Professor of Afro-American Studies
Betty Haven, Chair of Undergraduate Physical Education Department

ADMINISTRATION:

John W. Ryan, Former President
Edgar Williams, Vice President
Sarah McNab, Registrar
Joanne Bolen, Assistant to Registrar
Pam Flowers, Records and Admissions in Physical Education

IU STUDENTS:

Dan Burgess, Undergraduate
Stephanie Walker, Undergraduate

WRITERS:

Bob Hammel, Author; Editor of the *Herald-Telephone* (Bloomington, Ind.)
Joan Mellen, Author

Selected Bibliography

Appenzeller, H., and C. T. Ross. "Minnesota — Will a Bachelor of Arts Degree Affect a Career in the National Basketball Association." *Sports and the Courts*, Winter 1983, 9–11.

"Athletes and Academics." *Alpha Beta — Honorary* 2.2 (March 1989): 1.

"Athletes Measure Up in Graduation Rates." *NCAA News*, 8 July 1987, 1, 24.

Atwell, Robert H. "Some Reflections on Collegiate Athletics." *Educational Review* 60 (Fall 1979): 367–73.

Axthelm, Pete. "The Shame of College Sports." *Newsweek*, 22 September 1980, 54–59.

Benagh, Jim. *Making It To No. 1.* New York: Dodd Mead & Co., 1976.

Billick, Dean. "Still Winners." *National Collegiate Sports Service Bulletin*, 1973.

"The Black 'Dumb Jock': An American Sports Tragedy." *College Board Review No. 131*, Spring 1984.

Blann, F. W. "Intercollegiate Athletic Competition and Students' Educational and Career Plans." *Journal of College Student Personnel* 26 (1985): 115–18.

Bostic, D. "A Comparison of the Problems of Black and White College Athletes. " Unpublished manuscript, University of Florida, 1979.

Bozich, R. "Is Knight Mellowing or Bending Own Rules?" *Courier-Journal* (Louisville, Ky.), 20 December 1988, F1, F3.

Brede, R. M. "The Education of College Student Athletes." *Sociology of Sport Journal*, September 1987, 245–57.

Brunt, S. "Faking the Grade, Recruiting Scandals, Uneducated Players Are Price of Success for Sports Programs at Some U.S. Colleges." *Globe and Mail* (Toronto), 30 November 1985, D1–D2.

Champion, W. T. "Hall v. Minn.: Sport v. Studies." *Pennsylvania Law Journal Report*, 12 April 1982, p. 1.

"Classroom Comes First for Student-Athletes." *Indiana '88*, 81.

"Commission's Study of Student-Athletes Released." *NCAA News*, 5 December 1988, 1, 16.

Cramer, Jerome. "Kappan Special Report — Winning or Learning? Athletes and Academics in America." *Phi Delta Kappan*, May 1986, 1–8.

"Curing the Ills of Big-Time College Athletics: 22 Sports Figures Give Their Prescriptions." *Chronicle of Higher Education*, 4 September 1985, 75–76.

Dunkin, Zach. "Joe Hillman. I.U. Leader Says Baseball Can Wait... Until April." *Indianapolis News*, 16 January 1989.

Edwards, Harry. "Educating Black Athletes – NCAA's Rule 48." *Educational Digest*, January 1984, 22–25.

———. "Professor Blasts Educators and Blacks for Athletes' Lack of Academic Ability." *Jet*, 1 September 1986, 21.

———. "Getting That 'Mickey Mouse' Diploma." *Sporting News*, 23 February 1987, 16.

England, David. "Athletics, Academics, and Ethics: An Interview with Bob Knight." *Phi Delta Kappan*, November 1982, 159–65.

Ewing, L. W. "Career Development of College Athletes: Implications for Counseling Activities." *DAI* 36 (1976): 7204A. (Va. Polytechnic Institute and State University).

Falls, Joe. "Knight: Praised by Peers for Team's Achievements." *USA TODAY*, 25 January 1989, 7C.

Farrell, Charles S. "Turning Academic Rejects into Students Who Also Play Top Basketball." *Chronicle of Higher Education*, 25 March 1987, 36–38.

Feinstein, John. *A Season on the Brink*. New York: Macmillan, 1986.

———. *A Season Inside*. New York: Random House, 1988.

Forman, Ross. "Hillman's Seen the Good and the Bad." *Terre Haute Tribune-Star*, 5 February 1989.

George, Thomas. "Indiana Strengthened by Setbacks." *New York Times*, 13 March 1989, C1, C5.

Gerdy, John R. "No More 'Dumb Jocks.'" *College Board Review*, Spring 1987, 2–3, 40–41.

Gladwell, M. "Dunk and Flunk – Scandals of College Sports." *New Republic*, 19 May 1986, 13–15.

Graham, Andy. "Indiana Shuts Off Ellis, Sutton." *Herald-Telephone* (Bloomington, Ind.), 21 December 1988.

Hammel, Bob. "Cellist Starker Draws Parallels to IU Basketball." *Herald-Telephone* (Bloomington, Ind.), 21 February 1985, 13.

———. "A Knight with the Students." *Herald-Telephone* (Bloomington, Ind.), 29 October 1986.

———. *Beyond the Brink with Indiana*. Bloomington: Indiana University Press, 1987.

———. "Knight's Degree-Scholarship Plan Keys Symposium." *Herald-Telephone* (Bloomington, Ind.)

Hanford, George H. "Controversies in College Sports." *Educational Review*, Fall 1979, 60.

Harrison, James H. "Intercollegiate Football Participation and Academic Achievement." Paper presented at the Annual Meeting of the Southwestern Sociological Association. Dallas, April 1976.

Heyman, Ira M. "NCAA Forum." *NCAA News*, 8 July 1987, 6.

Humphries, Frederick S. "Academic Standards and the Student Athlete." Paper presented at the Annual Forum of the College Board, Dallas, Tex., 1983.

Indiana '89. Indiana University Athletic Department publication, 1989.

"Indiana's 'Deficiencies.'" *Sporting News*, Editorial, 21 November 1988, 40.

Kindred, Dave. "Knight's Virtues as Coach and Man Put Lapses in Shadow." *Washington Post*, 11 December 1980, F1.

Klitgaard, R. E. "Strengthening Academic Standards in College Athletics." Unpublished manuscript, Harvard University, John F. Kennedy School of Government, Cambridge, 1983.

——. "Possible Improvements in Proposition 48." Unpublished manuscript, Harvard University, John F. Kennedy School of Government, Cambridge, 1984.

Indiana University Basketball—A Winning Tradition. Bloomington, Ind.: IU Department of Intercollegiate Athletics. Booklet, 1988.

Lapchick, Richard. *Broken Promises*. New York: St. Martin's Press, 1984.

——. *Fractured Focus—Sport as a Reflection of Society*. Lexington, Mass.: Lexington Books, 1986.

——. *On the Mark—Putting the Student Back in Student-Athlete*. Lexington, Mass.: Lexington Books, 1987.

Leary, W. "The Billion Dollar Ripoff of Black Athletes." *Ebony*, Spring 1984, 153–54.

Lederman, Douglas. "Players Spend More Time on Sports Than on Studies, an NCAA Survey of Major-College Athletes Finds." *Chronicle of Higher Education*, 7 December 1988, A33–A38.

Leonard, W. M. "Exploitation in Collegiate Sport: The Views of Basketball Players in NCAA Division I, II, and III." *Journal of Sports Behavior*, March 1986, 11–30.

McDonough, Will. "Knight Says No to Hall." *Boston Globe*, 3 November 1988, 43, 45.

McPherson, B. D. "Black Athlete: An Overview and Analysis." Conference on Sport and Social Deviance, Brockport, N.Y.: 1976.

Mellen, Joan. *Bob Knight: His Own Man*. New York: Donald I. Fine, 1988.

Michener, James A. *Sports in America*. New York: Random House, 1976.

Naism, M. "A Failed Game Plan—College Sports and Black Youth." *Commonweal*, 10 April 1987, 199–200.

National Collegiate Athletic Association. *1986 Division I Academic Reporting Compilation*. Mission, Kans.: NCAA, July 1987.

——. *1987 Division I Academic Reporting Compilation*. Mission, Kans.: NCAA, July 1988.

Ness, R. Garry. "Academic Problems in Intercollegiate Athletics: Questioned Assumptions." *Journal of Physical Education and Recreation*, January 1981, 23–24.

Nichols, Mark. "What Price Glory? The Demands of Big Money College Sports Are Forcing Many Student Athletes to Spend More Time Studying Playbooks Than Textbooks," *Indianapolis Star*, F1, F6.

Nightingale, Dave. "Big Tension in Big 10 Scramble." *Sporting News*, 13 February 1989, 10.

——. "Controversial Late Knight with Hoosiers." *Sporting News*, 13 February 1989, 11.

Nyquist, Edward B. "Win, Women, and Money: Collegiate Athletics Today and Tomorrow." *Educational Record* 60 (Fall 1979): 374–93.

Oates, Bob. "The Great American Tease: Sport as a Way Out of the Ghetto." *New York Times*, June 8, 1979, 32.

Odenkirk, James E. "Intercollegiate Athletics: Big Business or Sport?" *Academe* 67 (April 1981): 62–66.

Purdy, Dean A.; D. F. Eitzen; and R. Hufnagel. "Are Athletes Also Students? The Educational Attainment of College Athletes." *Social Problems*, April 1982, 439–48.

Raney, J.; T. Knapp; and M. Small. "Pass One for the Gipper: Student-Athletes and University Course Work." *Arena Review*, November 1983, 53–60.

Renick, J. "The Use and Misuse of College Athletes." *Journal of Higher Education* 54 (1974): 542–52.

Rhatigan, James J. "Serving Two Masters: The Plight of the College Student-Athlete." *NASPA Journal*, Summer 1984, 42–47.

Ruden, Eric. "Senior Spotlight — Joe Hillman." *Hoosier: The Indiana Athletic Review*, 9 March 1989, 122.

Sack, A. L., and R. Thiel. "College Basketball and Role Conflict: A National Survey." *Sociology of Sport Journal*, September 1985, 195–209.

Sanoff, Alvin P. "Behind Scandals in Big-Time College Sports." *U.S. News & World Report*, 11 February 1980, 61–62.

Scott, Jack. *The Athletic Revolution*. New York: Free Press, 1971.

Sherman, John. "Bobby Knight's Strategy Scores in Business and Basketball." *Indiana Business*, November 1985, 28, 30, 34.

Shriberg, Arthur, and Frederick Brodzinski, eds. *Rethinking Services for College Athletes*. San Francisco: Jossey-Bass, 1984.

Smith, H. C. "Personal and Academic Characteristics of Black Athletes in NCAA Division I Universities." Ph.D. thesis, University of Pittsburgh, 1977.

"Some Are Making the Grade." *USA TODAY*, 4 April 1988, 2C.

Sowa, C. J., and C. F. Gressard. "Athletic Participation: Its Relationship to Student Development." *Journal of College Student Personnel* 24 (1983): 236–39.

Spander, Art. "Can Sports Tear Down Racial Barricades?" *Sporting News*, 13 February 1989, 5.

Spivey, D., and T. A. Jones. "Intercollegiate Athletic Servitude: A Case Study of the Black Illinois Student-Athlete." *Social Science Quarterly* 55 (1975): 939–47.

Stone, Jesse, Jr. "Black Colleges Threaten to Quit NCAA." *New York Times*, 13 January 1983, 1.

Strasemeier, Scott. "Making an Impact — Meeks Is Causing Trouble for Guards around the Big Ten," *Hoosier Scene*, 27 January 1989, 3.

Sutton, Stan. "Drugs Bench Indiana's Jay Edwards." *Sporting News*, 26 September 1988, p. 51.

Tackett, Mike. "Knight Demanded Facts: 'If You Lied You Were Gone.'" *Chicago Tribune*, 15 December 1978, sec. 5.

Underwood, J. "Student-Athletes: The Sham, the Shame." *Sports Illustrated*, 19 May 1980, 36–45.

U.S., Congress, House. *Oversight on College Athletic Programs*, 98th Cong., 2d sess., 26 June 1984.

Webb, Harry. "Social Backgrounds of College Athletes." Paper presented at the National Convention of the American Alliance for Health, Physical Education and Recreation, St. Louis, Missouri, 30 March 1968.

Zingg, Paul J. "Advising the Student Athlete." *Educational Record*, Spring 1982, 16–19.

Index

ABOUT THE AUTHOR

ROBERT P. SULEK recently graduated from Harvard University with an Ed.D. in Higher Education Administration and Social Policy. Having taught mathematics and coached basketball at both the High School and College levels, his lifelong driving force is the moral, social, and ethical issues behind basketball. Currently he works as Rector of the Honors College at the historically Black Johnson C. Smith University in Charlotte, NC.